TAKE
ROOT

HOW THE BEATITUDES REVEAL THE
ASTONISHING NATURE OF GOD'S GARDEN

LAURA A. MILLER

For more information, questions for reflection and small group study guides, visit www.takerootbylauramiller.com. With these resources, *Take Root* easily adapts into a 10-week study on the Beatitudes that is accessible to tweens, teens and adults.

First paperback edition July 2023

Cover art by Elize C. Watkins. Tree illustrations by Doan Trang. Chapter artwork by Kaitlyn, Ryan, Reid & Elise Miller or used under license from Shutterstock.com.

ISBN 979-8-218-21037-3 (paperback)

— DEDICATION —

To Drew, for showing me what it looks like to rest in God's love and for always encouraging me to write.

To my church, Resurrection Presbyterian, for the teachings and friendships that opened my eyes to the wonders of the Gospel.

Kaitlyn, Ryan and Reid, may the words that follow magnify your love for God and His kingdom. My love for you is poured out on these pages.

— MAJESTIC BEINGS —

Trees are very majestic beings,

Yet they get passed by and are not seen.

They are gentle giants, filled with peace,

A ready shelter for those in need.

Like kings they display their crown of leaves.

They are filters for sunlight, softening the beams.

Each grows waist-deep in history,

Holding memories in their many rings.

And though they're rooted in one single scene,

They never dwell but keep progressing.

Yet what I love most about these trees

Is that no matter the number of hardships received,

They stand up tall and keep their roots deep.

A poem written by Kaitlyn Miller

— THE BEATITUDES —

Matthew 5:1-12 NIV

Now when Jesus saw the crowds, he went up on a mountainside and sat down. His disciples came to him,[2] and he began to teach them. He said:

[3] "Blessed are the poor in spirit, for theirs is the kingdom of heaven.

[4] Blessed are those who mourn, for they will be comforted.

[5] Blessed are the meek, for they will inherit the earth.

[6] Blessed are those who hunger and thirst for righteousness, for they will be filled.

[7] Blessed are the merciful, for they will be shown mercy.

[8] Blessed are the pure in heart, for they will see God.

[9] Blessed are the peacemakers, for they will be called children of God.

[10] Blessed are those who are persecuted because of righteousness, for theirs is the kingdom of heaven.

[11] Blessed are you when people insult you, persecute you and falsely say all kinds of evil against you because of me. [12] Rejoice and be glad, because great is your reward in heaven, for in the same way they persecuted the prophets who were before you."

— CONTENTS —

— INTRODUCTION —

If you're a reader who feels stuck in the middle, between the rows of illustrated *Storybook Bibles* (too childish!) and the theology section (just too boring), this book is for you. It's written for teens/tweens but, frankly, if your age falls anywhere in between nine and ninety, you may want to read this to gain a better understanding of what it means to live for God's kingdom. There's no doubt God's Word is enthralling at every age and stage but to relate to it, you sometimes need a new vantage point that meets you where you are. I hope you, dear reader, find that in the pages to follow.

Let's start with somewhere we've all been: those little years when mornings were spent in footed pajamas and evenings barefoot running in the backyard. I knew God made the sunrise and then at night lit up the sky with stars. He was a good God but distant, like a school principal, looking after things behind-the-scenes so they would run smoothly. Of course, every Christmas and Easter I heard

miraculous stories of the virgin birth, a bright star in the East, an empty tomb, and the resurrected Jesus. The images burst on to the scene like an action-packed movie trailer recapping God's great drama. We played our part, decorating the tree, swapping gifts, dyeing Easter eggs and hosting big family gatherings.

Every December and April, in those moments, I sensed we were part of something BIG, that God was not far off but far more loving than I had imagined.

But, after all the decorations came down and the normal hum of life resumed, the volume turned down on God's grand Story. "So I guess that was it," I'd think to myself. People stopped listening as intently. We had seen the big idea – was there anything else to know? The rest of the year at church played out like the "fluffier" parts of a movie with lots of dialogue and side scenes, where even if you snuck away for a snack or checked your phone, it seemed you probably wouldn't have missed much.

And that's exactly how I learned the Bible. Over and over, I heard the climactic part of the story where God miraculously saves me from a final death. But I never quite saw the "middle part" about how I was supposed to live. Was it worth turning up the volume on God's *whole* rescue story? What else did He promise? What did it look like to play out His themes of wonder and love in all the side-

stories, even in my normal day-to-day?

When I was nine, I started going to Sunday school with that very question in mind. I sat cross-legged among the other fourth graders dressed in collared shirts and ruffled dresses, fidgeting with our hand-me-down dress shoes, uncomfortable in fancy clothes. Behind us was a row of 3-pronged hooks with several pretty charts and posterboards plastered above. And on the opposite wall, hung a large felt board displaying the eight Beatitudes from Matthew 5. All the "bee" attitudes converged on a conical hive, little smiley-face bees buzzing at the edges: "Bee-merciful, Bee-a-peacemaker, Bee pure in heart, Bee-cause that's how God will bless you!" Our teacher smiled and gestured to the "hive of happiness" as she spoke of Jesus' teaching.

It all sounded like godly advice but the whole vibe felt like a chore chart on my mom's fridge. What's more, this God was way off-character from what I'd seen in the thrilling "gospel preview" recapping Christ's birth and resurrection. This God was there to guide and lead me; but if I messed up, He was surely going to circle my name

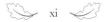

in a thick red marker and tell me "Shape up!" This was the distant school-principal-God of my little years, not the intimate, loving God I glimpsed at Christmas and Easter. I slouched down in my seat; how could I make sense of the two? Was this grumbling God (upset I couldn't quite live up to standards) really the same one that sat center-stage on Christmas and Easter, bidding me to come and be a part of His miraculous story?

Decades later, I discovered the Beatitudes WERE, in fact, Jesus' answer to how we should live. It's just that He didn't speak them as a task-master or as a list of to-dos. And He didn't speak them as nice rules to live by just to "Bee kind!" Rather, understood correctly, the Beatitudes ARE a picture of what it looks like to capture the fascination of Christmas and Easter, and let that same power play out in every facet of ordinary life. It is the *whole* picture of Christ's saving story – not just in death but in life.

Wondrous things like the virgin birth and the resurrection overturned the whole natural order of things and, likewise, the Beatitudes are a marvelous overturning of the natural order in our little lives. The gospel is, after-all, God's great rescue plan for eternal life beginning *right now.*

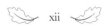

Not just in death, but in every fine detail of daily living. If we truly want to live as a child of God, we must learn how His extraordinary truths affect our ordinary day.

All our stories are part of God's great drama! And not just the action-packed parts, but the relatively boring moments of our lives: sitting in class, going to practice, washing the dishes. We exist within His Story, and it is the Beatitudes that highlight the role we are to play in our ordinary 24-hour day. Even Jesus, God Himself, had His plan advance between sleepy nights and slow mornings, among average people eating, drinking, bathing and cooking. The dull moments matter to God. And as the Spirit works within us day-to-day, Christ is remarkably unfolding the last chapters of His promise to redeem and restore His creation.

Read along to discover the Beatitudes and how ***a tree*** (rather than a bunch of buzzing bees) is a robust, scripturally based image to remind us of our part of God's story. Trees, as it turns out, exemplify how to grow in Christ. Said another way, if we wanted a script for the role we are to play in God's story, we need only to look at the life of a tree.

It is certainly no coincidence that trees string together the gospel from Genesis to Revelation. In fact, other than God and people, the Bible mentions trees more than any other living thing. Watching a seed or sapling grow into

a mighty tree, weathering the seasons and elements and bearing fruit, is a complete metaphor for a life full in Christ. It is an example of how we should live for God, translating the high points of the gospel into everyday living and growth in Christ.

After reading this book, you'll see that tree outside your window as more than a collection of branches and leaves. It will be a reminder of God's ways and how He wants us to live as part of His Story and as part of His kingdom. You'll notice His great drama unfolding in and around you, even in the normal, everyday things. Your life will be a part of the glorious tale of man and woman getting back to the garden, the new Eden, to live eternally with God, just as He always intended. You'll find in this garden many trees always in bloom, bearing fruit every season, never withering but rooted by streams of living water.

And at the center is Christ, a new, perfect Adam, ruling perfectly over God's garden, nurturing the tiniest seed of faith – yours and mine – into a tree that brings Him glory.

1

— GRAND (RE-) OPENING OF — GOD'S GARDEN

On the corner in my neighborhood where I grew up, there was a sleepy auto shop with never more than one or two cars in the lot. Its two garage doors stayed shut like the eyes of a dozing giant. We zipped by it every morning, but it was lost in the concrete landscape – a forgotten stop between Weigels, where we got Icees, and Kay's, where we got ice cream.

Thirty years later, driving by with my own three kids in the backseat, our attention was caught by a bright red banner with white lettering. "Grand Opening!" it read: something new had come! This once sleepy, quiet spot was boasting a great announcement. We pulled over to peer into the window, hands cupped over our eyes, foreheads pressed

against the glass. The signage inside read "Pop's Donuts" and what we saw was better than we ever could have imagined: trays of cake and yeast doughnuts, blueberry, maple-glazed, fruity pebbles, Bavarian cream and chocolate glazed!

When we think of Jesus' ministry, we can also see it as a sort of "Grand Opening." More accurately, it's a "Grand

(Re-) Opening" of the garden. "God's kingdom is Here!" Christ declares. "Leave your silly little kingdoms and be a part of Mine! Be a part of My Story!" If Christ had a banner, it would have read "The kingdom of God Has Come!" After all, the announcement that God's kingdom is here, that God's garden has been re-opened through the work of Christ, is the cord that ties all of scripture together (John 14:6)! And this is what Jesus talks about more than anything else in the gospels.

Now, the word "kingdom" can seem strange at first. Shrug off any ideas of crowns, thrones or scepters, no glimmering swords or gallant knights. God's kingdom is not a specific place but rather the reality of God's rule and reign – everywhere and anywhere, in any corner of life. Its center is within each of us who believe and receive. It's within His body, the church. In essence, it is wherever believers are co-ruling with God, doing things His way, to play out His story in the everyday events of our lives.

Jesus' announcement of His public ministry didn't include streamers, sidewalk chalk or vinyl banners. Instead, He declared it with very little fanfare to a crowd sitting huddled together on a grassy hillside. In the eight Beatitudes, Jesus sets forth His way of living: an invitation to come and live God's way. It was His own way of describing how He wanted His followers to be and to live. He spoke the Beatitudes, not as a list, but rather as a picture in broad strokes of what life should look like in the kingdom of God, back in the garden, with Him in charge.

But, unlike Pop's Donut Shop, Christ's Grand Opening wasn't always met with smiles and happy customers.

Jesus' words flew in the face of all the bigwigs, the hotshots and all those powerful people that had been in charge ever since the fall in Genesis 3. The Romans saw His promises as an attack on their non-religion that treasured status, power and comfort. "The important thing is being important!" they'd say. "Follow Jesus and you'll amount to nothing!" As for the Jewish Pharisees, they took Jesus' words as an attack on their religion that valued rules, traditions and moralism. "The good life is about being good!" they argued. "Follow Jesus and you'll never live up to our standards!"

The gospel of Jesus, meanwhile, promised much more and made it much easier. "Love Me, love others and you'll be more loved than you could ever imagine. It is not about living up to standards. It isn't about keeping rules, about being good or about trying harder. It is about trusting Me in all things."

So, instead of a grumbling parent or a moral teacher, try to think of Christ more as a revolutionary. For just like a revolutionary, He questioned and overturned the existing values of society. His words went out like bombshells, blowing up the audience's ideas of what it meant to be "good." Jesus' message was radical but simple, announcing that the garden had re-opened and anyone could, once again, be in His presence. Faith was all that was required! He was not leading a military revolution but one of the heart – one that is still underway, advancing in bits and pieces, person by person. The glorious garden we glimpse in Genesis 1 is being re-built on broken people finding new life rooted in Him.

From Wilderness to Garden

As a family we like to watch Tennessee basketball together. Dressed in bright orange t-shirts, we shuffle into

our seats and wedge in between fans just as the lights go dim. The same pump-up song echoes in the stadium. The scent of popcorn, Petros, and hotdogs with ketchup (and that green stuff – mushed up pickles?) fills the air. As we listen, we begin to settle into the familiar ... we've been here before. And it's happening again. Here come the players, running onto the floor, spotlights crisscrossing the court. Another chapter for the team is about to unfold; the story is about to continue ...

Jesus did the same thing using garden imagery. He wove a little trail of garden images throughout scripture that all believers can follow, from beginning to end. The word pictures announce, "It's happening; God is coming!" The garden, as we know it, equates with God's presence. And the end is meant to tie into the beginning, the trial, the cross, and the victory: the Garden of Eden, the Garden of Gethsemane, the tree (cross) on Golgotha and the Garden in Revelation. Anytime you see garden imagery, you know the great Gardener is on the scene.

It's like a little primer for your brain: a "get ready, here we go again!" It's a visual that cues you into His great narrative of hope, His great rescue story.

It was God's plan, after all, all along, from the very beginning, for human beings to walk with Him and rule over

5

creation. In the first two chapters of the Bible and the last two, God's people are in a lush garden living perfectly under God's rule. The end of the Bible loops all the way back to the beginning, back to how God planned for it to be! And it is Jesus who restores us to our place in the garden and teaches us what it looks like to live as part of His kingdom.

More specifically, the Bible begins and ends with the Tree of Life, in Genesis and Revelation. It symbolizes God's presence and His promise of eternal life. Now, this tree shows up in the book of Proverbs, among others.  Here, wisdom itself is the tree of life. Growth in wisdom is understood as growth in knowing God and in knowing ourselves. So, scripture tells us it is possible to experience this tree *now* by being in relationship with Him, and by growing in wisdom.

So think of it this way: the tree of life, the presence of God, is now in us. Jesus, the new Adam, is gardening the whole earth for the glory of the Father. In the new Eden, WE are in God's presence, fed by the living water of Christ, the great Gardener. The same Spirit we see in Genesis chapter 1, hovering over the earth to bring light and life, is the same Spirit still at work, hovering over our lives to bring about wisdom and goodness. No one is too far gone or too unworthy to become a planting for the all-new Garden of Eden God is building for eternity.

As a result, Jesus often used the image of a flourishing tree in His garden as a metaphor for a life rooted in Him. Using such symbolism was a creative way of teaching those that believed, that truly listened. See for yourself what these scripture verses say:

- Psalm 1:3: "You're a tree replanted in Eden, bearing fresh fruit every month, never dropping a leaf, always in blossom."

- Luke 13:18-19: "How can I picture God's kingdom for you? What kind of story can I use? It's like an acorn that a man plants in his front yard. It grows into a huge oak tree with thick branches, and eagles build nests in it."

- Proverbs 11:30: "A good life is a fruit-bearing tree."

- Hosea 14:4-6: "I [God] will love them lavishly… He'll put down deep oak tree roots, he'll become a forest of oaks!"

Don't you find all of that so refreshing? And you are part of that picture. You are like a sapling of the Spirit that God grows to make you more like Christ. And it is the Beatitudes that explain what the Spirit is doing within you.

In the chapters that follow, I will take you through the Beatitudes, their meaning and how each ties into the Bible's imagery of a tree. So tuck this book and a blanket under your arm and choose a tree in your yard. Find shade beneath its canopy, leaning your back against its sturdy trunk, legs outstretched over the knobby, deep-running roots reaching down and out. Touch the rough bark and listen to its leaves shutter and its branches sway, bending but not breaking. Watch how it puts out leaves year after year, even after cold, harsh winters. It is humble and dependent and yet purposeful and magnificent.

In God's garden, we ARE a tree such as this, reliant on Christ to bear fruit, and magnificent in His glory. Isaiah the prophet wrote, "They [that's us] will be called oaks of righteousness, a planting of the Lord for the display of his splendor" (61:3, emphasis added). God is once again delivering His people from the wilderness but this time He is going to turn the wilderness into a garden. He's taking all the dry and desolate places and turning them into a fruit-bearing garden (Isaiah 32:15). Because you see, the gospel story is not only about how Christ came to save you from a final death, but how He graciously also promises you a fruitful life, starting here and now.

> That person is like a tree planted by streams of water, which yields its fruit in season and whose leaf does not wither—whatever they do prospers (Psalm 1:3 NIV).

Blessed are the poor in spirit

— SEEDS OF FAITH —

*Blessed are the poor in spirit, for theirs
is the kingdom of heaven.*

Matthew 5:3 NIV

very tree begins with a seed, miraculously bringing
forth new life seemingly out of nothing. For this
reason, a seed perfectly captures Jesus' ideal of
"poor in spirit." As C.S. Lewis said, "Think of yourself just
as a seed patiently waiting in the earth: waiting to come
up ... in the Gardener's good time, up into the real world,
the real waking."[1] This is where God's great tree metaphor
begins to paint a beautiful and helpful picture. From the
outside, a seed is just a hard little nugget of cells. Nothing
to show for itself. You can buy them dirt-cheap by the
hundreds at Ace Hardware or Lowe's. But that is exactly

how God would have it. He likes to start with nothing so that all the amazing growth that follows (the sturdy trunk, thick branches, canopy of leaves and heavy fruit) is all credited to Him. It is all for His glory.

Worldly wisdom can lead us to think just the opposite – as if entering into God's garden will be more like the end of a cross country race. You've run up hills, dodged rocks, pushed through mile after mile, and then, phew! – you spy the crowds huddled around the finish. You trudge the final feet to the finish line and some chipper mom throws a medal around your neck, directing you to the bins of lemon-lime Gatorade and bowls of bananas. You made it! All because of grit and determination! Beaming parents give you a pat on the back "Well done, buddy!" "Way to stick with it, sister!" Man, all that hard work paid off!

But "poor in spirit" is a complete reversal of this triumphant scene. For "poor in spirit" is best translated as having nothing to offer or "being at the end of our rope" (Matthew 5:3). It refers to that runner still stuck at the starting line, barely able to put one foot in front of the other. Turning out his pockets, empty-handed, he shrugs, "I've got nothing."

As Christ would have it, this person who has nothing to offer is the very one that is welcomed at God's garden gate. "Blessed are the poor in spirit, for theirs is the kingdom of heaven" (Matthew 5:3 NIV). God knows that only by realizing we're really quite helpless can we see we're in need of the Helper.

Living a life of dependence on God translates into "less of you and more of Him" (Matthew 5:3). That is ultimately what it means to be poor in spirit. Jesus takes helplessness, something we're all trained to loathe and avoid, and makes it the pathway to His kingdom! We are to bring nothing to the table. He wants us to be God dependent, not self-dependent. All my inked-up planners, tidy to-do lists, reports of good grades and records of "Well done!" "Congrats!" fall flat at the feet of God. If anything, my busyness is a sign I'm not relying on Him.

Jesus put this Beatitude first perhaps because it reminds us at the very beginning not to see His teachings as just another list that we hurry to complete. Instead, the Beatitudes are a total upheaval of "the norms," meaning the worldly standards we normally expect, and a return to how God wants us to live, with Him in charge.

You understand the norms of your house or school where your parents or the principal is in charge. It's how things "work" to live peacefully and happily together. You clean up your own messes, you wait quietly in the hall, you write your name in the top right corner, you don't slam  doors and dad always gets the extra crescent roll. But in God's kingdom, the norms take quite a different form. First, nothing is required; there are no "to-dos." You don't have to prove your worthiness or bring something to the table. You just come with your heart. Jesus was announcing a fundamental change in how the world would work.

To understand His teachings correctly though, you must see the Beatitudes as meant for all Christians (not just the super-spiritual but people like you and me). And all of them apply, all the time. In other words, it is not up to your teacher to be "meek" and you to be the "peacemaker." Or, for you to be mournful on Mondays and merciful on Fridays. No, all eight should be part of our character, all the time. So, taken together, the eight Beatitudes describe a model citizen of God's kingdom.

And there is a spiritual sequence in the Beatitudes, in the sense that they build off each other. The Lord didn't just haphazardly make a list but rather teaches it in a definite order: the first four are about loving Him, the last four are about loving others. This is because we all first need mending on the inside before we can love others. Or in the words of C.S. Lewis, "You cannot love a fellow creature fully till you love God."[2] As new creations in Christ we should be different from what we were, having an entirely new way of life and a new attitude. It is the way of life in His garden, in the new Eden: first, love God and then, love others (just as it is written in Matthew 22:37-39).

Now, right off the bat, "poor in spirit" reminds us we can do none of this on our own. We come to God like those rigid, flat, dry animal sponges that you plunk in the tub and watch grow ten times their original size. We are empty but we grow and reach our fullness by immersing ourselves in Him.

But it's easy to get swept up in that proverbial race to the finish that is so much a part of our culture. It's that serious "get 'er done" vibe all over school, work and even in our home. The idea that all our rushing-about determines our self-worth was a lie I bought into early on. I was caught up in the kingdom of this world, not the kingdom of God. There is perhaps no statement that highlights the rub between the two more than "Blessed are the poor in spirit." While the world would have us rely on status, wealth, personality or good behavior, God would have us to rely on Him. We come with empty hands. He doesn't want us chasing little kingdoms when we have THE Kingdom.

Just read the reports from those who have, by the world's standards, made it to the finish line they set for themselves. They finally got whatever they were running after, but here's what they have to say:

- A multi-millionaire New York banker: "It's not enough."

- Two-time Golden Globe winner actor, Jim Carrey: "I dream of being a three-time winner, then maybe I'll finally be enough … and I could stop this terrible search."[3]

- A struggling singer that finally has a breakthrough performance: "I used to think 'If only I could make it!' But now I'm unhappier than I used to be." [4]

These examples don't rule out hard work and determination. Those are values to live by as certainly God doesn't promise everything should be smooth sailing! But believing we ARE enough in Him gives us the courage to say "Enough!" to our endless striving to become something outside of Him. You no longer feel you have to try so hard to be someone when you already know you are a child of God (1 John 3:1a). Your identity is in your reliance on God, not in your success.

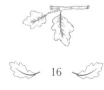

Jesus was so passionate about this first Beatitude that He taught on it again, and again, and AGAIN. In Luke 14 and 15, teaching in the house of a very important Pharisee, Jesus presents a string of parables illustrating this surprising truth of the kingdom of God. They are meant as a warning to the proud who see no need for God, and as an encouragement to the lost whom Jesus came to find.

Just imagine all those fancy-pants Pharisees gathered around a table with Jesus, looking smug and superior, their spiritual "to-do" lists all checked off. Then Jesus nearly knocks them off their chairs with His upside-down kingdom invitation: "When you have a banquet, invite the nobodies, the poor among you" (Luke 14:13). The Master's banquet will be full of people such as these (Luke 14:21). Those that are so obsessed with their own fussings and doings will never be God's disciples, He explains (Luke 14:33). You must first give up your own kingdom in order to enter into God's.

"Geez, how low can He go!?" the Pharisees must have muttered. Was Jesus truly welcoming the low-lifes and the good-for-nothings among them? Was He really grasping for the hands of the empty-handed?

In the next chapter, Luke 15, Jesus goes on to progressively show just how much God loves the lost and dependent. The parable of the Lost Sheep, the Lost Coin and the Lost Son all showcase God's delight over a repentant believer who sees his need for God. "This brother of yours was dead and alive again; he was lost and is found" (Luke 15:31). He embraces his son and then, without being asked, the father puts a robe around him (protection), sandals on his feet (sonship), a ring on his finger (authority), and celebrates his homecoming (Luke 15:22-24). The message is clear: we bring nothing to God. We are lost and then found. We must first be emptied before we can be filled with His abundance.

Well, this was quite a jolt to the listening crowds. They had all been in training for the big race – you know, the one where God pats you on the back at the finish line and directs you to the snack table. But Jesus shows us that finding God is not the result of trying harder. Rather, it's like that moment, lying still in bed, you find yourself awake. [5] You know that moment when your eyes open and you realize it's morning? You don't work at it; it just happens as you open your eyes and see the light. That tiny sliver of sunlight that first peeked through the curtains is now streaming in, casting a warm glow on even the darkest places. So not only do you see the light but, by it, you see everything else!

And God works like this. Requiring nothing of us, He wants to pour out His grace and truth on us until it seeps into every corner of our lives. By keeping our gaze on God and letting His love for us filter through everything, we become poor in spirit. The more we see ourselves and this world as they truly are – stuck in the darkness – the greater our dependence on the true light, God Himself.

Let's come back to talking about seeds. Tree seeds also start out dark and dormant. But scientists know that this state of dormancy, though it looks like a time of rest, is actually a time when the seed is changing on the inside. Germination, when the little seedling pops out, is simply the first time we have evidence of all this change on the outside.

And so it is with us, as God's children, as trees of the new Eden. God first works within us, unseen, changing our hearts and minds. He breaks open our hard shell and brings forth new life. We awake to this new reality, seeing and recognizing for the first time His great light and love and our need for Him. We come up into the real world, into His kingdom.

We may call it repentance, conversion or, even better, a break-through moment. But God sees it as the budding work of the Great Gardener, His Son Jesus. Through His death and resurrection, Jesus overcame death to now have the power to bring life in us (1 Corinthians 15:54-56). We are the trees of the new garden, sprouting up to ultimately bear fruit for His glory.

How can God do this – bring riches out of nothing or, in plainer words, life out of death?  Remember the upside-down, topsy-turvy nature of all the Beatitudes? The wondrous work of Christ that began on the cross is still working to overturn the natural order of things. He is reversing our natural, fallen tendencies so that we might again live in His presence – fully. "It stands to reason, doesn't it, that if the alive-and-present God who raised Jesus from the dead moves into your life, he'll do the same thing in you that he did in Jesus, bringing you alive to himself?" (Romans 8:9-11).

After Jesus' death and resurrection, Mary Magdalene was the first person to see Him. Crying over His empty tomb, she saw Jesus approaching her but she did not recognize Him in His resurrected body. Instead, she supposed Him to be the gardener. And, indeed He is the gardener, not of ordinary seeds and plants, but of His people![6] Jesus is restoring the garden, one seed at a time, one soul at a time, to bring all glory to His Father. And you, as a child of God, are a seed of His garden, wholly dependent on Him.

3

— LIFE FROM BARREN —
BRANCHES

Blessed are those who mourn, for
they will be comforted.

Matthew 5:4 NIV

I t's quite remarkable that every Spring a tree must start all over, making leaves from empty branches. It's a massive undertaking that requires energy and effort. Just think how it feels when you've worked for hours on a school project and then mid-sentence your iPad freezes up. You re-boot and find the paragraph written yesterday in study hall, but the pages that followed have all disappeared. Your cursor blinks against a white, empty screen. Letter by letter, you begin to recreate. And such is the life-cycle of a

tree, losing its entire canopy in winter to then start over in the spring. Leaf by leaf, the tree must rebuild.

But like the tree, by experiencing loss we feel more deeply the joy of being complete. Wouldn't you agree, finally turning in that paper is more satisfying *because* you had to painstakingly draw it out of a blank page? In the same way, the lush green of every Spring is so glorious *because* it bursts out from the barrenness of winter. Without experiencing emptiness, we wouldn't know the joy of being filled. Each accentuates the other in being its opposite. And God intended for all His creation to understand both, together, so the great work He's doing is evident.

We come to Him like blank pages, asking God to use us to write His story. But we cannot, with our whole heart, desire for God to make things right, unless we first accept that we and the world we live in are empty and broken without Him.

I remember exactly the moment I began to understand the world was a broken place, needing to be put right. It started in the elementary cafeteria. At the center of my lunch was a PB and J on white, made with smooth peanut butter (because that nut texture is gag-worthy at age six) and goopy strawberry jelly, oozing out at the edges. On the side were little baby carrots wrapped in cellophane and a tiny

Tupperware of ranch dressing for dipping. And at the bottom of my lunchbox, hidden under a napkin, was a Halloween-size Twix leftover from the stash my mom had bought for trick-or-treaters. Linoleum at my feet, wedged between friends, it was a grade A first-grade lunch.

But later that afternoon my tummy felt off. I was riding my bike up and down my long driveway when I felt my hands get sweaty and the blood drain down from my face. I rolled off into the grass, threw down the handlebars and hunched over. This was my first meeting with that terrible nemesis: food poisoning. If it hasn't happened to you yet, odds are it will, and you'll find yourself longing for the time when sickness will be no more (Revelation 21). Just that wee bit of ranch dressing gone bad offered a vivid picture that things are not as they are meant to be. This world, including sickness of all kinds, needs to be put right. Knowing this, grieving this, makes us more eager for God's power and presence to burst on the scene, wiping away pain and evil once and for all, even vile food poisoning.

My husband, Drew, had his moment at a much younger age. He was riding in the Oldsmobile with his mom in what used to be a common parent-child ritual: running errands

(back in the day when you had to get everything at a real STORE). At a stop light, he lunged forward, pointing out the window, "Mommy, why is that bunny broken?" The bunny lay on the side of the road, ear flopped over his eye with his hind leg stiffly distorted. Even his young eyes could see that something was not right. Drew didn't recognize death or call it by name but he knew that outside his window a life had been dealt a drastic blow, seemingly for no reason at all.

No matter how it happens, from the moment we see things aren't right, we long for them to be made right. This is what it means to "mourn" as Christ meant it. We should mourn over our own brokenness and the brokenness of the world around us. Usually at some point in childhood you realize things aren't always rosy. You get sick, someone hurts your feelings, you do something wrong, you lose someone or something important to you. But mourning is not about moping around with a pouty lip or waking to a pillowcase wet with tears. Mourning, biblically, is about seeing and recognizing the sin in and around us, and desiring that one day we and this world will be mended and made whole.

We can look to Jesus to provide the only true way out of brokenness and darkness. Again, He teaches the Beatitudes, not as a list of "to-dos" or "how-tos," but as a description of life in His garden: this is what it looks like to live as a child of God. A famous preacher over 150 years ago, Charles Spurgeon, described the Beatitudes as a "ladder of light" to deep happiness.[7] Like rungs in a ladder, the second Beatitude follows the first. You've read about how "poor in spirit" is an emptying so God can do the filling. You understand how in the face of God's holiness, we come with empty hands, with nothing to offer. Knowing this, it's quite natural then that I will mourn over my helplessness, my sin and all the "ickiness" in and around me. "Why isn't that fair?" "Why is there COVID, anyway?" "And why do my grandparents have to keep growing so old?" You might even mourn over things inside of yourself too. Like "Why did I slam the door on my sister?" "Why am I not able to be nice to that person?" "Why do I feel like I'm not enough?"

Everyone wants to find the answers to these questions and fix the brokenness in and around us. We spend hours, days, weeks, even years, trying to patch ourselves up and hide these faults and icky feelings. Just walk into any bookstore and the biggest section is Self Help. Adults line the aisles, thumbing through pages, looking for a way to deal with all the unkindness, confusion or fear they feel day-to-day. All the books have the same theme: "We can do this if we just try harder! If we just show some stick-tuitiveness!" Short-cuts to happiness cheerfully chirp off the pages, sounding pleasant and full of promise. "Relax!" "Eat Right!" "Be confident!" "Find balance!" "Smile!" or (my favorite) "Buy something fancy!"[8]

But the Beatitudes offer something radically different. Jesus isn't laying out a catchy eight-step program or formula to fix our brokenness. For scripture tells us there's no way *we* can deal with our brokenness/sinfulness on our own. Even the good things we do are spoiled when our motive is how nice it will make us look or how more likeable we will be. There's just no hiding or covering up our self-centeredness because ALL our life is tainted with sin. Think of it like this: if sin were the color red, we'd be red all over. Different parts of our personality would be different shades of red: scarlet, crimson, ruby, rose, blush, maroon, and so on. But every last inch of us, including everything we say or do, would be tainted red.

In this Beatitude, Christ is therefore calling us to recognize our brokenness, so God – not we ourselves – can make things new. Remember, God is working in a different way: He welcomes our emptiness and our brokenness so that He may be glorified for His work in us and in this world.

There is an ancient proverb about a young girl whose morning chore was to walk to the river to fetch water. On a pole, resting across her back, hung two pots: one was perfect but the other was cracked. The little cracked pot, feeling empty and useless, asked the girl one day on the way home from the river, "Why do you keep using me when all I do is leak?"

Smiling, the little girl responded, "Have you seen how the flowers flourish on your side of the path? Every day you water them. What you thought was a flaw, is actually a gift."[9]

Brokenness is an invitation for Christ to occupy more of our lives. Everyone, whether we recognize it or not, is unworthy before God. But this second Beatitude asks us not to try to hide it or fix it with all our short-cuts or ten-step plans. Rather, it is important to be honest about our brokenness, to mourn about it so we are driven ever closer to God. Our weaknesses, failures or "cracks" in our character are the openings God needs to do His work. Where there is mourning, He offers hope.

Jesus, being fully human as well as fully divine, experienced the full range of feelings and emotions that we

go through: hunger, tiredness, pain, grief (Hebrews 2:17; 4:15). So, even though He was without sin, He still mourned over the brokenness of this world. He openly grieved about death and the pain it causes. Picture Him weeping over the death of His friend, Lazarus, as He sat and shared in the sorrow of His friends, Martha and Mary, Lazarus' sisters (John 11:35).

In a similar way, the scriptures also tell us that Jesus "wept over" the city of Jerusalem. Drawing near the city's gates, He mourned over all the people within who didn't recognize Him for who He was (Luke 19:41-44). Ignorance and unbelief had blinded their eyes to the truth. So they failed to see that right before them their King, their Maker, was riding in on a colt to rescue His people. In this instance, the cross was just days away and Christ was dreading what He knew would have to take place (Luke 12:50). But Christ's experience of grief brought the reason for the cross clearly into focus.

Have you noticed that in all the superhero movies, the camera scans the broken city before zooming in on the hero's last saving act? We're shown all the destruction the evil villain has carried out before the rescuer comes on the scene. And, in the same way, a broken world was the only backdrop for Jesus' great act of redemption. But the important thing to realize is His times of mourning motivated Him to endure the struggle set before Him, never losing sight of the joy that was promised beyond the cross (Hebrews 12:2).

Like us, trees find new life only against the backdrop of emptiness and brokenness. Every winter, as the air grows cold and daylight shortens, trees let go and shed all their leaves. What a sorrowful and humiliating state, being reduced to a web of branches and twigs! One can almost imagine the tree is mourning the hardship and emptiness of winter with its branches barren for months.

But look closely at that winter tree outside your window, the same one you ran beneath barefooted in the summer finding shade. Because, even now, with its leaves browned, withered, and piled at the curb, you notice your tree is ornamented with something small and round. Produced by the tree in late summer, these buds are the promise of next year's leaves, blooms, and branches. They offer visible hope even as the cold sets in, for the joy of next spring has already been promised! Every leaf and branch of the tree grows from such a bud at the tip of a twig.

Likewise, we too are caught up in this cycle of mourning and joy. We feel the cold brokenness of the world and we sense we are barren and empty with nothing lasting to offer. But, as Christians, we are immediately comforted. He never gives up on us, instead He gives us signs of hope. He is growing us and extending our understanding of Him. When we see these things in ourselves, we know the Great Gardener is undeniably at work, making good on His promise to bring new life out of the old.

The power of this promise is rooted in His Son Jesus in the most unlikely way. You see, Jesus is not pictured as a towering oak but instead, as one humble, solitary shoot! The prophet Isaiah likens Him to a stump – a young, green shoot from a low, lifeless-looking tree (Isaiah 11:1). As God was rebuilding His new garden, He chose to start with one tender twig! And in His great power, He strengthened this root from Jesus' forefather Jesse to bear the fruit of mercy and love for us all. He did this to show that nothing is too far out of His reach or too far gone. Out of one tiny shoot – that's also you and me – He can build a massive tree for His glory. There is no circumstance too bleak or too hopeless to keep God's grace from bursting forth in us.

And, because Christ went before us with the humblest of beginnings, we can be confident God will work in us. He is tending to His garden until that glorious day when there will be no more mourning. All the unkindness, confusion, fear, death and sadness will be wiped away. Forever! From then on, the trees of His garden will be beautiful and always green (Genesis 2:9; Jeremiah 17:8). They will always be flourishing, never losing their leaves, bearing fruit every month of the year (Revelation 22:2). Anyone that believes in Him and surrenders their life to Him will be like those trees, forever joyful for the work He's done.

Blessed are the Meek

4

— BENDING, NOT BREAKING —

Blessed are the meek, for they will
inherit the earth.

Matthew 5:5 NIV

Strong storms or winds cause trees to bend and sway. Like a pendulum in a clock, their branches and leaves swing back and forth to the rhythm of the howling winds. Think about it. If a tree were to stand rigid and straight, large limbs or even the trunk could easily snap. But by bending it does not break. Of course, strong gusts of wind may strip off the leaves; but that does not matter as long as the tree remains rooted and whole. So it survives, not by resisting the storm, but by surrendering to it. This is Nature's portrait of meekness.

And Jesus desires the same for His people. He wants us to be humble, mild and responsive, willing to lose even our crowning glory to follow Him through life's storms. By being rooted in Him, the meek have the power to *absorb* the brunt of criticism and insult, confident in our place in God's kingdom.

Every night I lie under the plaid quilt, my son's head resting on my chest, with our dog Millie lying at our feet, her muzzle propped up on a stuffed alligator. Teeth brushed, PJs on, shades drawn, I smile at the familiarity of it all as we end our day the way we've always done – in the pages of a book. We've read through some of our favorite funny ones lately; story lines that include parents that seem oblivious to all the goings-on under their roof.

Rhinos Don't Eat Pancakes and *One Cool Friend* are bestsellers that both tell the tale of a child hosting a strange houseguest – a large purple rhino or an Emperor penguin – right under the nose of out-to-lunch parents. Over and over, the kids try to tell their  mom or dad but NOBODY LISTENS.[10] Meanwhile, the purple rhino eats pancakes in the kitchen and the penguin devours all the anchovy pizzas. They sit on the couch, take a bath and even ice skate in the bedroom; but STILL, the supposed big-time busy parents don't take notice.[11] The children are the only ones that have the pleasure of witnessing the extraordinary.

Preaching to the crowds, Jesus was like a big purple rhino on the mountainside. Imagine the Savior of the world walking right in the midst of people going about their daily lives! But the big, busy, *important* people just couldn't see Him. Instead, it was the lowly, the ordinary and the overlooked that heard His proclamation of a new, upside-down kingdom. Like the children in our bedtime books, they trusted and delighted in the presence of this surprising visitor: the true God, in human form (Matthew 19:14).

It was to this small circle of believers that Jesus offered the shocking promise in the third Beatitude: "Blessed are the meek, for they will inherit the earth."

Who are the meek? It's not necessarily those kids in class that seem so naturally kind and easy-going all the time – those that don't care if you cut in front of them in the lunch line or borrow their markers and never give them back. And it's not those that always talk in a small, soft voice. No, being meek goes much deeper than just personality. A meek person is a portrait of strength under control. They don't get easily worked up but are rather quick to listen and slow to speak. However, though they are often the ones pushed aside – the ignored, the invisible – they aren't spineless pushovers. They instead have a sense of deep contentment, enabling them to absorb wrongs, cruelty and unkindness, and trust in the Lord's ways.

In our modern day, examples of meekness are rare (it's like ice cream for breakfast – doesn't happen often). I was on a summer trip to the mountains of Montana when, unexpectedly, God gave me the best example of meekness, as Christ intended it.

Straightening myself in the saddle, I heard a hoof scrape on a rock kicked up on the wooded trail. I ducked to

 avoid a mess of needles and sap and stretched my neck to see beyond to the line of horses ahead. We were on a short outing on horseback, just for the fun of it since it was my son Reid's first time riding. Fred, Reid's horse, was amazing – completely loyal to his new four-foot tall master, curbing his strength and yielding to the rider's commands. He was gentle, obedient, and *meek*. In the original Greek, "meek" (*praus*) is often used to describe

such a trained horse (the Greeks trained their stallions for battles, not trail rides! But still …). These horses kept their fierce spirit and courage but had been trained to respond to the slightest nudge. They could be at a full gallop at 30 miles per hour and then come to an abrupt halt at a word. Or in this case, at the slightest tug from a six-year-old.

We are to be meek in this way as we live in the kingdom of God. A meek person isn't so puffed up on their own important plans that they miss God's cues. Instead, they are teachable, mild and responsive, trusting in His will. Like a reined horse, they stop at His word and only move ahead at His encouragement. They take that unexpected turn or go through rocky patches if that's where He's leading.

An interesting tell-tale sign of the meek is that they worry less about what others are saying or thinking about them. They are confident in God's leading and don't get wrapped up in others' approval which, in turn, allows them to absorb criticism. Insults, put-downs, or attacks on their reputation don't harm them as they did before. For, if you let the truth of God's love get BIG – so big that it comforts you, guides you and thrills you – then you find that criticism loses the power to claim any hold on you.

In this sense, the third Beatitude is a step up from the first two – if you remember Spurgeon's ladder. If being "poor in spirit" and "mourning" is about realizing our helplessness and need for God, then being meek is allowing others to see that too.[12] This is very difficult – to say the least! It's one thing to say of myself, "I've got nothing!" but quite another to allow *somebody else* to say, "You've got nothing!" But that's the peculiar truth of the gospel: anyone that intends to follow Christ must come empty-handed in order to follow His lead (Matthew 16:25). For the meek aren't showy and proud, but open and responsive. They roll all their hurt, insecurities, and doubts onto God, trusting He is the perfect provider (He knows just what we need), and He is the perfect judge (one day He will make all things right).

You can think of it also like riding an ocean wave.

If we stubbornly try to stand in our own strength – upright, proud and defensive – the surf repeatedly knocks us off our feet and we are swept under, clambering to get back up. However, if we trust enough to pick up our feet and hold out our arms, we are carried. Rolling our lives, our cares and our reputations onto the Lord, we don't resist the strength of the tide but instead ride it into shore. We rest in His love, and trust where He's taking us and, as a result, the waves lose all their power to bowl us over. We emerge on firmer ground, and though we may stumble, we will not fall, for the LORD will uphold us with His hand (Psalm 37:24).

This is exactly how Jesus lived His life. Though He was God, He never tried to be independent of the Father to determine for Himself the steps of His life (Philippians 2:6-7). Rather, Jesus was wholly dependent on the Father for direction.

> "I'm telling you this straight. The Son can't independently do a thing, only what he sees the Father doing. What the Father does, the Son does" (John 5:19-20).

Christ's astounding ability to self-deny power and yield to the Father's plan is the highest example of meekness. He is the epitome of strength under control. He could have allowed harm among those that sought to kill Him and He could have had a legion of angels rescue Him from the fate of the cross! But He was obedient; He was meek. Jesus instead absorbed all the horrible hurt, unjust punishment, suspicion, jealousy and hate, and rolled them onto the Father.

When they hurled their insults at him, he did not retaliate; when he suffered, he made no threats. Instead, he entrusted Himself to Him who judges justly (1 Peter 2:23 NIV).

Outside of Jesus, there is only one other person described in the Bible as meek: Moses. He confronted Pharaoh, led his people out of Egypt, and endured forty years in the wilderness. Yet he described himself as "very meek, more than all the people who were on the face of the earth" (Numbers 12:3 ESV). The Israelites envied his position, spoke against him, and were ready to lead a rebellion against him. Even his own brother and sister turned against him! But Moses, though he had every reason to, did not resent it, made no complaint to God and did not confront them. Instead, when his sister Miriam was punished by God for criticizing him, he asked for God to heal her (Numbers 12:13). This wasn't because he was a mousy, shy, timid pushover! No, it was because he was a man determined to live out God's will, even at the expense of his own pride.

Scripture tells us Moses stayed the course, looking ahead to his reward. For that he is highly praised along with many others such as Noah, Abraham, Sarah, Joseph and Rahab (Hebrews 11). God had planted in all of them a seed of faith that grew into a giant oak because of their trust.

It was a trust in a love so BIG that they endured bullying, betrayal, mocking and mistreatment, and at times lived friendless, homeless and powerless (Hebrews 11:38). Like a mature oak in a storm, they absorbed the changing winds of circumstance. They remained stable amidst cruelty and chaos, for they knew God had a plan to make them fruitful for eternity.

These examples of kingdom living totally reverse the way of thinking we are accustomed to. Just turn on the TV and it's all about having hordes of friends, a lovely home or a fancy title. "Look at how I made this ... bought this ... got this ... earned this!" We certainly can use our talents and gifts to bring God glory but, if we're honest, we also use them to say, "See, I'm a somebody, not a nobody!" We hold tight to these marks of "being good," "being known," or "being right" to feed our ego and pride. We adorn ourselves with achievements just like a tree embellishes itself with leaves. (Scientists call it the "crown" of the tree; we call it our "crowning achievements!") The way we might look at a tree's leaves to identify it (an oak, a maple, a pine or poplar), is like putting out our good works and saying, "Tell me who I am! Am I an artist, a scholar, an athlete?" Like a single tree dressed in thousands of leaves, we are a display of all our "good works."

What could these good works be? How about: our good grades, the winning goal, hours of volunteer work, a painting, a project? What about a string of followers on social media? Yes, we do all we can to hang onto our emblems of pride. But, deep down, we know any identity we make for ourselves outside of Christ can be easily shaken like the leaves on a tree by a storm or changing winds.

Take the star high-school athlete who in the first game of his senior year leaps to catch a TD pass but crumbles awkwardly on his defender. The pop he heard in his left knee is the sound of a college scholarship down the drain. Or what about the popular girl who once had a Facebook following of hundreds but, after a careless comment, she finds herself friendless. Not only does she have no one to sit with at lunch, she's embarrassed to tell her mom she's being bullied over some careless text. You get the picture. A failed test, a fumbled pass, misunderstandings, mistakes and missteps can leave a person feeling completely empty and broken.

But the gospel offers a beautiful truth: "Give up yourself, and you will find your real self. Lose your life and you will save it." C.S. Lewis in his book *Mere Christianity* then goes on to explain, "Submit with every fiber of your being, and you will find eternal life. Keep back nothing. Nothing that you have not given away will ever be really yours." [13]

In a gust of wind or in the darkness of winter, a tree will shed its leaves, letting go of its crowning glory. And in our life, undoubtedly, at some point, Christ will ask the same of us. A dark or hard time will strip away our source of pride and, if we are wise enough, we will let it go and follow His plan. That is the picture of meekness. By letting go of our self-sufficiency, we are able to absorb the cutting remarks of others. By letting go of our sources of pride, we are no longer broken by the biting wind. By shedding all our attempts at being good enough, we resist the storms of insult. For a barren branch easily sways and bends and will not break. And in the end, the tree endures, and the storm even serves to strengthen its foundation at the roots.

This was what happened to Moses, Noah, Joseph and other giants of the faith. When they let go of their pride, offenses could roll over and off without upending their trust in God. As a result, their faith grew. During hardship they didn't break because they surrendered to God's plan. Like a tree in a storm, they absorbed the harshness, trusting in more good to come in the right season.

We are ONLY able to do this because Jesus went before us. He faced, not just a harsh word or trial, but the horrible storm of God's fierce anger at sin – our sin. All the sadness and brokenness of the *whole world* was poured onto Him. Stripped and nailed to a felled, lifeless tree, He absorbed ALL the wrongs that were ever done and will ever be done against God. All of it, every last insult, attack, abuse or offense. "Christ redeemed us … by absorbing it completely into himself" (Galatians 3:13). He took the penalty of it all. In this ultimate display of meekness, He suffered in silence, content to let God set things right (1 Peter 2:21-25).

At Jesus' death, the whole sky turned black – like a bruise. All the hurt and sadness we rolled onto Him, He absorbed on that day. That is how we know we can confidently give all our mistakes, wounds and doubts to Him. He doesn't react or fling punishment back at us. He doesn't condemn us or rebuke us.

Instead, His grace overturns the whole natural order of things by absorbing the consequences of our sin so that we never have to. He took our place and faced the fiercest storm of all eternity! Jesus was not just some surprise visitor. He was the Savior of the world, destined to re-open the gate to God's garden so that we could forever flourish and, one day, live totally at peace, never having to face a storm again.

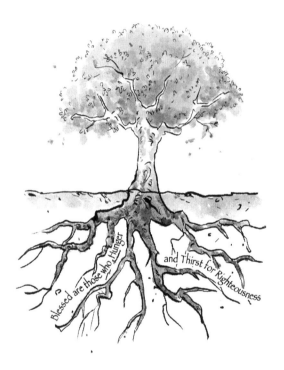

5

— EXPANSIVE ROOTS —

Blessed are those who hunger and thirst for
righteousness, for they will be filled.

Matthew 5:6 NIV

A tree's roots are always growing, reaching deeper and stretching wider to soak up nutrients and to support itself in the ground. It is this firm and solid foundation upon which everything else grows and flourishes. A tree has the main root, the taproot, that grows directly downwards from the seed. Similarly, it's our faith that immediately roots us in God (Colossians 2:7). Everything we long for flows through Him. Like a mass of underground roots, our faith grows hidden from view to support and sustain us through every season. Christ bids us to explore the depths and width of His love, promising one day we will be firmly rooted, filled and no longer craving the things of this world.

Do you remember as a child how amazed you were by just plain-old reality? Things such as water dripping down a windowpane or an earthworm wiggling in the dirt equated to top-notch entertainment. We were thrilled to watch the world unfold and be drawn in by our imagination.

But, as we get older, the simple facts just don't cut it. "Seen that before!" "I want something cool, not ordinary!" Once upon a time, we used to gaze at water rippling over creek rocks, an elephant's large trunk or the bright yellow center of an egg, totally fascinated. But now we want more. Calm waters no longer thrill, so we seek out raging rapids; bored with zoo animals, we plan a safari to see the more exotic; and tired of our usual two eggs sunny side-up, we order the fancy French take on eggs benedict. You get my drift?

We seem to always be craving for something new, something novel, the next best thing. We're continually after that something to captivate our heart and leave us feeling satisfied. "If only _____, *then* I would be happy, *then* I would be filled." And, on and on the cycle goes, churning out masses of adults longing for the bigger house, the latest

gadget, the better job, the coolest vacation, only to get it, and then the shininess wears off. "Well maybe just one step further" they reason. "That house with the saltwater pool, that phone with the uber-mega pixel camera, that job with the fancier sounding title, or that beach with the perfect white sand."

Take, for example, the middle-school band teacher Joe in Disney's movie *Soul*. Even after he nailed the big gig he'd been pursuing his *whole* life, he was surprised he STILL felt empty. The entire theme of the movie seems to point to the fact that nothing in this world can fully satisfy us. But, here's the strangest thing: that was DISNEY, not Sunday school. Even non-Christians acknowledge the feeling of emptiness within us. And, left to ourselves, none of us can ever quite shrug off that feeling.

The only logical explanation, as C.S. Lewis proposed, is this: "If I find a desire which no other experience in this world can satisfy, the most probably explanation is I was made for another world."[14]

And so we were! We were MADE for God's kingdom. Everything in creation, in this world, is just a pointer to the

Creator. God says, "You want to be satisfied? Everything in this world only awakens wonder, leaving you thirsting for more. The *only* newness that lasts is being made new in Me!"

This fourth Beatitude is the pivotal point in Jesus' teaching. "Blessed are those who hunger and thirst for righteousness, for they will be filled." "Righteousness" refers to our right standing with God through Jesus who made it possible. What led up to this verse are all descriptions of emptying ourselves. We come with nothing, saying, "My problems are far beyond me" (poor in spirit), "I desperately need help" (mourning) and, "Lord, you need to take over" (meekness). Now, in our emptiness, we immediately look to be filled.

And this IS the crucial moment. Many of us might run through these first three Beatitudes and then – feeling hollow – try to do everything we can to fill ourselves back up! "Yes, Lord, I need You because I can't stand feeling empty! Just help me with that test or give me that win on Friday night and *then* I'll be satisfied." We feel desperate, worried, distressed, and so end up pleading for a morsel of "good" to tide us over.

We do the same when we physically hunger and thirst, chasing down anything to stop our stomach from growling. We'll chow down on that half-eaten, smushed cheeseburger on our brother's plate. Or even take a swig of dad's black coffee or that weird Kombucha stuff, if we have to. The feeling is hard to ignore. "Mom, really, I'm going to die …" you explain from the backseat, begging for a snack. Annoyingly, she keeps on with that line that must be in all mom manuals: "You'll have to wait for dinner." Finally home, that first morsel of food from your plate is marvelous – you were empty but now you're filled; you were longing but now you're satisfied.

That's exactly how God wants us to feel when we come to Him. Jesus welcomes us, saying, "Come to me desperate. Work up a good appetite for God!" (Matthew 5:6, modified). "Don't snack on the things of this world. Stop nibbling at the breadcrumbs when the greatest, most amazing spread has been prepared for you!" All "the good" we chase after – maybe it's being the best baller, winning class competitions or scoring a spot on student council – all these are like little finger foods, meant only to awaken your appetite for the true feast. But they can never fulfill. And, if we continually munch on these snacks, then we will hardly rejoice when the real feast is served!

So in this fourth Beatitude, Jesus is calling out to us: "Just as your body craves delicious food and drink, so does your soul need ME. Seek My righteousness – not your own self-righteousness. Desire to be with Me and you'll find true lasting happiness. I am the Living Water that can fill you. I am the Bread of Life that can satisfy."

All of mankind (we're not the first) has found it terribly difficult to rely on God's promises and provision. We fixate on what we don't or can't have. We get caught in that loop "If only ___, then I would feel complete! Why is God keeping that one thing from me?" We might think it's because of something we've said or done, but from the beginning God withheld things from mankind. Think back: why did Adam and Eve insist on eating from the one tree that was off-limits? Tempted by the serpent, Eve sought wisdom, the "one thing" Satan convinced her would make her complete and ultimately like God (Genesis 3:4-6).

Adam and Eve's grave mistake was they sought the good stuff God gives us, not God himself. We too seek provision, but fail to delight in His presence. We want a good house, a stocked fridge, a fun vacay, a time of relaxation, but it all fails to fulfill if we don't have Him. For, just as it was in Eden, we were designed to dwell and walk with God. "Seek

 54

me first, fill up on me," God says, "and I will give you it ALL, including eternal happiness."

God deliberately withholds good things as a way to instruct us to treasure Him above all else. When He refuses to give us the good thing we are begging for (which are just crumbs at His table), He is actually giving us something even greater: His presence (a feast for our souls!).

A more intimate illustration of this truth is in the story of the Samaritan woman at the well (John 4). Do

you remember it? The woman is feeling sad and bummed out and so she goes to fetch water mid-day when she knows she'll be alone (everyone else was at home dodging the blazing heat). But, surprisingly, Jesus is there and speaks with her (because He's always showing up where people need Him). And, bit by bit, He reveals her physical thirst is really just a symptom of her deeper spiritual thirst.

Yes, she feels parched and worn out but, even more so, her soul is withering. All her life, she has been chasing after that "one thing" she thinks will complete her, repeatedly filling her bucket with new affections, hoping to draw up something that truly satisfies. But her well can never satisfy,

no matter how many times she pumps the water. In her need to feel accepted, loved and filled, she has sampled the love of many men, but each one left her feeling dry and empty.

Jesus instead offers her a drink of *living* water – water that would become in her a "spring of water welling up to eternal life" (John 4:14 NIV). It would never cease, never give out. No more drawing up and drinking in the things of this world! Christ offered an endless flow of acceptance and grace. The woman responds with  curiosity and then with sheer delight like she had received the best gift ever! Running off to share the good news, she leaves her bucket behind because, spiritually speaking, it is no longer of use to her. Her new faith had loosened her grip on the things she'd once longed for and created within her an eternal spring that always satisfies.

It is the same now as it was then. Jesus is the source, the fountainhead, breaking through, pouring out an endless stream of love on all who believe. And so, when we feel empty and hollow, as if our soul has been scraped dry, we need only to listen to Christ's promise: if we seek Him, we will be filled. But, like this woman, we must first let Jesus ask of us:

"Where are you trying to draw up water? Where have you dug wells that you keep digging into? School, sports, friends, family? The coolest toys, the latest tech, clothing or cars? Stop digging!" He says. "Put down your bucket. Tap into Me and draw from My well! Be like a tree planted by streams of water. Grow rooted in My love for you" (Psalm 1:3).

Now a tree root is a hardy thing. It can grow in deep sand, under pavement and even on rock surfaces. And likewise, God can grow one's faith amid deep shame, doubt, and even firm opposition (think of the apostle Paul!). It starts small. It doesn't matter if the root shoots sideways, or whether it's puny, twisted or gnarly. What matters is its location – in His garden, in His kingdom.

From there, growth always continues. More roots branch out, slowly over time, edging outward and inching downward. From that first teeny-tiny root, a massive structure fans out beneath the ground. It is the tree's source of strength. After all, it is the roots that soak up moisture and minerals and provide support. Over the years, the root system grows to be wider and more far-reaching than even the tree's branches and leaves. And all this is happening underground hidden from view, in secret, beneath the surface.

Like a root system, our faith is always in "expansion mode" as there are no boundaries to God's love. The great Gardener bids us: "Reach out and experience the breadth! Test its length! Plumb the depths!" (Ephesians 3:18). Saturate yourself in His love and soak in His life-giving grace. Continually draw Him in. Just as roots enable a tree to stand against destructive winds and long periods of drought, the hidden roots of our faith dig deeper and spread wider, making us unshakeable in Christ.

Now, as in any garden, it is the Gardener God, who prepares the soil (or shall we say "the soul"?) and tends to our growth. But there is a sort of energy required of us too – we must "be energetic in [our] life of salvation, reverent and sensitive before God" (Philippians 2:12). It's true we cannot create righteousness, we can't just produce it; but we can put ourselves in places where we might get it. So, get near to God. Gaze upon His truths. Read your Bible, go to church, spend time in prayer, and hang out with people who sharpen your faith. There's a lot of truth to the saying "You're the average of the five people you spend the most time with." So surround yourself with the wise. Resist filling up on the "good things," dulling your hunger for a life with Christ. You will become like a thirsty tree planted by the water, multiplying its roots to draw it all in.

And you'll be amazed – for this water will never run dry, no matter how much is drawn out. It flows from a never-ending stream of God's grace as we see in Psalm 1. And just as He offered it to the Samaritan woman, He offers it to you.

Christ, again, is the one that makes all this possible. He endured great thirst on the cross so we would never thirst again. He took what we deserved and paid the ultimate price for all the ways we look to be satisfied outside of Him. He became dry as a bone and was poured out "like a bucket kicked over and spilled," so that our bucket would always be full when it comes to His love (Psalm 22:14).

For a moment, Christ was even willingly uprooted from His source of living water and cast away from God. Though it can be hard and confusing to think of God turning away from Christ in His very time of need, we must see its good purpose. Sin cannot exist in God's presence. Christ endured the separation from God we deserve, so that *we* can be confident we will never be abandoned. He went through all this so that WE could be replanted right back in God's garden. On that day, hanging on a cross, Christ thirsted so that we could be eternally saturated in God's love, fixed forever by the clear crystal waters of the river of life flowing from the throne of God (Revelation 22:1). [15]

6

— INTERMISSION —

The massive red velvet curtains unfold and close over the action on stage. The orchestra plays its last note and the musicians rest their instruments. It's now intermission in this piece on the Beatitudes – a break between Act 1 and Act 2.

So, let's do as we do in the intermission of the Nutcracker or your sister's school musical. Once the lights switch back on you turn and, drawing in a deep breath, ask "Well, what'd ya think?!" Time to chat and summarize all we've seen in Act 1. (Also, if you've been reading this straight through – which would be amazing – it's a good time to grab some popcorn or those delicious little Junior Mints).

First question: "Okay, so exactly what are we to make of these Beatitudes? Is this Jesus' version of an eight-step program?"

Actually, no! Quite the opposite: God would have us bring nothing. His emphasis is always on *being* over *doing*.

He cares much more about our attitude than our actions. We are to come to Him feeling worthless, helpless and with empty hands. Having realized the need, we hunger and thirst, and then God comes with His wondrous answer – a life rooted in Him. But God does the planting. He prepares the ground. For some, His truths are like a shovel driving into hard soil; for others, the soil is soft and fertile and the seed of faith is planted with little effort. If you've felt like "I've always been a Christian," the latter description is probably true of you.

When does this happen?

Many of us can't remember a time we were without God. Knowing Him at a young age, it was if we were begun from a seed or sapling. Though our faith was small, He was already at work in us. Others are like transplants, uprooted from the life they were living, willing to lose all to gain a new life in Him. Either way, God works out of barrenness. We all come with really nothing of worth. And this is just where Jesus would have us: barren with nothing to give but a readiness to be rooted in Him.

This is where the great Gardener always begins His work: out of nothing. You see this all over scripture. God literally chooses the barren – Sarah, Rebekah, Hannah – and those with nothing to offer – Abraham, Moses, David – as the seeds and transplants for His kingdom.

Even all of creation was born out of nothingness (Genesis 1:1). And that same Spirit hovers over us, with the power to bring something out of nothing.

What's next?

Jesus' announcement of the "norms of His kingdom" has two parts. The first four Beatitudes are all about *where* our heart is planted (do you love God?); the last four concern *how* our heart grows (do you love others?). Or, put another way, the first four are how we become a Christian, the last four are how we live out this new reality with the Spirit working in us. We have to first be a Christian before we can act as Christians.

Here's a sneak peek. You'll notice beautiful parallels between the first four and last four Beatitudes. [16]

the 8 Beatitudes

1st Beatitude
Blessed are the poor in spirit

Knowing my problems are far beyond me,

2nd Beatitude
Blessed are those who MOURN

Knowing how much I need HIM,

I am more merciful towards others and their PROBLEMS

5th Beatitude
Blessed are the MERCIFUL

I try to serve him with all MY HEART

6th Beatitude
Blessed are the PURE in heart

3rd Beatitude
Blessed are the MEEK

able to meekly accept criticism

filled with his RIGHTEOUSNESS

4th Beatitude
Blessed are those who hunger & thirst for righteousness

I think less of myself and make peace with others

I can deal with hard things in this world

7th Beatitude
Blessed are the PEACEMAKERS

8th Beatitude
Blessed are those who are persecuted

See how God's beautiful, unexpected plan unfolds? He starts with nothing to bring forth life and love abundantly. It's all according to His will and design for His new garden, His new kingdom, that is slowly taming the wilderness until one day – one glorious day – when all will be made perfect.

So, let's get back to it: dim the lights, draw the curtains and turn to Act 2.

Blessed are the Merciful

7

— THE GIVING TREE —

Blessed are the merciful, for they
will be shown mercy.

Matthew 5:7 NIV

In his book *The Giving Tree*, Shel Silverstein tells the story of a tree with a voice to describe a life of merciful giving. From the beginning, the tree was happy to have a young boy as her companion. He ate the tree's apples, slept in her shade and swung from her branches. As the boy grew older, he wanted more. So out of love, she gave him her apples to sell and later her branches to build a tree house. Finally, she gave him her trunk to build a boat. In the end, the only thing left was a stump that the boy (now a very old man) sat and

rested on. The tree joyfully gave and was content just being with him. She was willing to give her all to the one she loved, just as Christ gave His all for the ones He loved. Christ calls us to the same merciful love, giving what we can to save others from suffering.

One of the most incredible real-life accounts of merciful love is recorded by Corrie Ten Boom. As a Holocaust survivor, she traveled around the world to tell how God's mercy empowers us to extend mercy to others, even to those we want to hate.

On this occasion, just months after the end of WWII, she spoke in a church in Germany. The silence was still thick with emotion. People were angry, grieving, sad and distraught. You could feel the weight of their emotions, like the heavy air that lingers after a big thunderstorm. But Corrie's healing words slowly seeped into the crowd, peeling back the darkness so light and life could stream back in.

After Corrie's speech the crowd quietly filed out of the back of the room. All except one German, who made his way forward, briskly walking towards her. Immediately she recognized his balding, heavyset figure. Just the sight of him picked up the storm in her heart. A gust of memories swirled, raining down all the details of her time as a Nazi prisoner.

Corrie Ten Boom was now face-to-face with the guard from the Nazi concentration camp where she and her sister, Betsie, had been imprisoned for illegally hiding Jews. Betsie never made it out; she died in the camp. And, by now the guard did not remember or recognize Corrie. So, after a quick, "Hey, hi, how are you?" he went on. "I have become a Christian. I know that God has forgiven me for the cruel things I did there, but I would like to hear it from your lips as well. Fraulein, will you forgive me?"[17] His hand thrust out waiting to clutch hers.

He was asking her to do the most difficult thing she had ever been asked to do: forgive the murderer of her sister. His hand thrust out waiting to clutch hers.

She knew forgiveness and mercy did not always come naturally but more out of will. So she willed herself to do it

– to stretch out her hand to grasp his. And, as she did, God's mercy flooded her soul like a stream of warm, bright light. The storm in her heart was stilled. It was then that Corrie Ten Boom deeply understood that every day her sins had to be forgiven by God and so, in turn, she was able to have mercy on this man who oversaw her sister's death. Her hand in his, she cried out: "I forgive you, brother! With all my heart!"[18]

By viewing herself as a sinner too like the German guard, Corrie chose to save him from the guilt and torment of all his wrongdoing. Instead of crying out in anger, she remarkably stretched out her hand in peace.

Jesus' teaching in the fifth Beatitude powerfully reads: "Blessed are those who are merciful, for they will be shown mercy." In the simplest of terms, mercy can be defined as "not giving a person what he deserves." It is an attitude towards others that flows out of the first Beatitude "Blessed are the poor in spirit." For the more we understand we come empty-handed before God (feeling desperate and unworthy), the more likely we are to extend mercy to others. Or, put in another way, the more we understand how God's mercy saved us from sin's terrible fall-out, the more we're willing to reach out.

Corrie's forgiveness was a *form* of mercy: giving up her right to get back at someone (even though he deserved much worse!). In any act of forgiveness, we have to let go of anger, resentment or bitterness. And true forgiveness (not just excusing it or putting it on the back burner) always comes at a cost to the one who is doing the forgiving. Corrie was willing to "forgive the inexcusable because God [had] forgiven the inexcusable" in her. [19]

We often think of mercy as a "big act." But it also shows up in how we relate to the nagging brother, the annoying friend, or the frustrated teacher. As we've seen, it's not just feeling pity or sending happy thoughts to that person. In every instance, it requires ACTION, big or small. For Corrie, this was an outstretched hand. For us, it may be holding our tongue (even though our brother is asking for it), eating lunch with a lonely friend (even though she deserves to be alone after what she did), or lending our teacher a hand (even though she just lost it in front of the class).

The "mercy-full" put pity into action, preventing further misery and hurt. Yes, we can all say "Oh poor thing ..." or "Bless her heart ..." but *doing* something is the next level. It's what Christ is calling us to in the fifth Beatitude: to be His hands and feet, to show mercy to others. Often it involves this idea of walking in someone else's shoes. This means we have to get right inside the other person's skin until we can see, think and feel exactly what they are going through. By doing that, we often realize we're not that far off and have maybe even felt that way before ourselves. It's called empathy. And having such empathy, we are then moved with compassion to lighten the burdens of others.

In the house where I grew up, there was a long green couch in the den, wedged right up against a big bay window. Since the window curved out, behind the couch was a teeny-weeny crescent shape retreat, just the right size for a little girl. I'd crawl back there undetected and wait, listening and watching for events to unfold around me. My mom chatting on the phone. My brothers crisscrossing the den, on the way up to their room or out the door. My dad reading the newspaper, zoning out after a day's work at the office.

There was something soothing about being in the midst of life, but not having to participate in it. No expectations, no guilt, no demands, as long as I remained quiet. My one-sided game of hide-and-seek eventually seemed childish (or let's be honest, one day my long legs no longer fit), so I ditched the routine. But, surprisingly, in this grown-up adult world, I found everyone still at play. Of course, no one is climbing behind couches or curling up in the cabinet, but many are instead hiding behind notions of "That's not mine to deal with," or "She probably just needs space," or "It'll work out as it's meant to."

We tend to stick to our own business and stay in hiding. The mantra is "You take care of you; I'll take care of me."

But that's not at all how Jesus sees us living in His kingdom. He wants us to be *actively* saving others from their suffering. He wants us to feel so deeply forgiven ourselves, that we're willing to forgive and give, even when it's costly. The spirit grows us until we no longer feel comfortable in our hiding places. He nudges us out to carry each other's heavy burdens and reach out to those in need. Even if we can't physically save someone from hurt, we can intercede for them knowing Christ continually does the same for us (Hebrews 7:25).

Now this idea of being "mercy-full" was an unsettling teaching for Jesus' listeners. Loving others, He warns, is way more important than keeping to ourselves, staying out of trouble, and maintaining an unblemished personal record (Matthew 9:13). But the culture of Jesus' day saw mercy as a flaw, not a virtue. To the Roman mind, being merciful was equated with being a weakling and could cost one their reputation! They glorified courage, justice, discipline and power, leaving little room for compassion. One Roman philosopher of that time even wrote "Mercy is a disease of the soul."[20]

The Jews (especially the high-ranking Pharisees) were just as wide-eyed as Jesus called them out for being driven by rules, not by love. "I'm after mercy, not religion," said

Christ (Matthew 9:13). And the Pharisees were religious all right, meticulously following a code of 613 rules, 248 commandments and 365 prohibitions.[21] But their hearts weren't in it (Matthew 23:27-28). Christ was offering a stern warning: religion without mercy is a sham, a fraud, a hoax. The Pharisees were all caught up in the rituals of religion, working so hard to be obedient, that they had no eye for hardship and no heart for compassion.

Jesus drove this point home in the story of the Good Samaritan (Luke 10:25-37). It begins with a Jewish man, beaten by robbers and left half dead on the side of the road, groaning out in pain to those passing by. A priest strides past and stops to pity his fellow brother but, feeling the pull of his all-so-important business in Jerusalem, decides to carry on. He reasons there is nothing he could do given his tight schedule: "Well, I just can't be late or, worse, touch the unclean… someone else can deal with it." Likewise, a Levite comes along and feels sorry for the man but his to-do list cannot accommodate any delay.

It was shortly after that a Samaritan traveled down the road. Now Samaritans did not mix with Jews, let alone lay a hand on them! Jews, in fact, despised Samaritans, viewing them as a mixed race with an inferior religion. But hearing the man in pain, the Samaritan came near to him and took pity on him. He brought him water and bandaged his wounds until the man was revived enough to ride with him on his donkey to a nearby inn. He then instructed the inn keeper to take good care of the Jew and gave his word to cover all the expenses. "Go, and do likewise," said Jesus (Luke 10:37). Of all three, who do you think showed mercy? Of course, only the Samaritan. He displayed a costly form of mercy that mirrors the divine form of mercy we see in Christ.

If that wasn't enough, Jesus shows the flip-side of this teaching in the parable of the unmerciful servant (Matthew

18). It tells of a man who owed his king a whopping $100,000 (that's enough to cover lunch at Chick-fil-A every day for 27 years!). Empty-handed, the servant came to his master and pleaded for mercy, "Oh please, pretty please give me another chance!" The king took pity, erased his debt and let him go.

Free and forgiven, the man went out on the street and bumped into a fellow servant. "Oh, hi there! YOU still haven't paid me that $10 you owe me! Fork it over, NOW!" he demanded, grabbing his friend by the neck. (Mind you, this guy just got 27 years of nuggets and fries and now he's going after one lousy eight-count meal!) The servant fell to his knees, begging for mercy. But the man refused. Of course, the king got wind of this and was outraged.

After experiencing that extravagant show of generosity, the wretched man had shown no change of heart. He never understood forgiveness. And so, that unforgiving servant was punished until he repaid the debt.

As I read these parables, my first thought is always "That's not me!" I could never saunter past a man in pain or, after being forgiven so much, turn on a friend for so little. But then come to think of it, I'm guilty of it almost every morning. Standing at the kitchen counter, I stew how it's me unloading the dishwasher again, collecting all the dirty laundry and laying down all my plans for the sake of others. Like the priest and Levite, I fight the inconveniences – a sick child, a hurting friend, a lonely parent – knowing it will all require a sacrifice of what *I* want to do.

We even try to keep score in the trivial things. Who last fed the dog? Who got the bigger piece of cake? Who was left to clean the bonus room? Like the unmerciful servant, we shout "You owe me!" forgetting that we are walking around free, light on our feet, only because the debt we owed our Father was wiped away.

Let's face it; if we're truly honest, we too still find Jesus' teaching on mercy profoundly radical. Like the Jews, we're willing to give as long as it doesn't draw too much on our pocketbooks or our plans. And, like the Romans, we turn a blind eye to someone in distress. Wanting to appear worthy and sufficient, the one with power or control, we don't like mingling with the weak. We divide the world into good and bad people, deserving or undeserving.[22] We constantly assess the situation and decide if it's worth disrupting our own busy schedule or digging into our wallet.

But Christ doesn't see it that way – He divides the world into those that know they need Christ and those that don't. And, while we might prefer to shuffle past and stay hidden, the Spirit calls us to come out to save others *because* we've been saved. None of us would naturally "go and do," truly loving their neighbor as ourselves. Sure, out of our own selfish motives, we might help someone out if it makes us look good in the end. But Spirit-driven mercy is quiet and unassuming – not fussy or flashy.

Jesus explains this later in the Sermon on the Mount: "When you do something for someone else, don't call attention to yourself … don't think about how it looks. Just do it – quietly and without being noticed" (Matthew 6:2-4). The fruit of a poor spirit is *genuine* mercy for others.

We could learn a lot from trees about mercy. Trees give quietly, without a murmur, saving the world around

them from hurt, shielding others from suffering. For the homeless, they provide shelter; for the hungry, they provide food. Trees house nearly half of *all* the creatures that live on land and their leaves provide shade for the tired and worn out. Wood from their branches and trunks is used to build homes, make furniture, magazines, candy wrappers and even cereal boxes![23] Tree sap gives us maple syrup, gum, crayons, paint and soap. We even get medicine from trees to help us when we're sick. And we snack on apples, peaches, pears, cherries and all types of nuts only because a tree drops them for the taking. The mere sight of a tree also nourishes our soul, gracing the landscape with its towering trunk and majestic, green, leafy canopy.

Think about how a tree reaches out its branches and roots, just like Corrie Ten Boom reached out her hand and just as Jesus wants us to reach out to others. Tree branches literally are gestures of mercy, saving us from harm by recycling the air so we can breathe. Without trees, we'd struggle in a cloud of our own exhales, full of carbon dioxide and low on precious oxygen. Leaves not only convert the CO_2 back to breathable O_2 but purify the atmosphere, catching and filtering harmful particles so we (and all the animals) can breathe easy. Roots also reach out to prevent erosion and help water the earth with rain, drawing in droplets from the soil to send to its leaves and eventually the air. Because of trees, water and rain can travel more than 300 miles inland, bringing life to otherwise dry areas.[24]

Like a tree, we function by drawing in and giving out. We can reach out, deal with the hard stuff and turn it into something beautiful. We can do this, rooted not in our own strength but, being poor in spirit, rooted in our need for God. It is a continual process of drawing in and giving out.

All of this, of course, is only made possible through Christ. He is the ultimate example of empathy, literally coming to earth as God to live in human flesh, entering into every detail of life (Hebrews 2:17). Even though He was misunderstood, mislabeled and mocked, He kept extending mercy to others – costly as it was. Then, in the end, on the cross, He did one final act that cost Him everything: He extended mercy to all. Hanging on a tree, arms outstretched, with very few looking on, Christ quietly yet profoundly saved all His people from the terrible consequences of sin. Even as they drove nails in His hands and feet, Christ turned to His Father asking, "Father, forgive them, they don't know what they're doing" (Luke 23:34). The cross saved us from what we rightfully deserve and, only by truly knowing that, can we extend genuine mercy to others.

8

— TREE RING PATTERNS —

Blessed are the pure in heart,
for they will see God.

Matthew 5:8 NIV

The heart of a tree never stops growing. Though their height is relatively fixed, trees continue to add width to their trunks throughout their life, year by year. As new layers are added, the innermost bands become denser and stronger, while the outer rings pump water and nutrients to every part of the tree, right to the tip of each branch. It is out of this inward, hidden center that a tree sends out sap to support the production of leaves and fruit. Some years the tree will appear to flourish; other years it may appear skimpy and sparse. But the heart of the tree is always growing and changing, no matter the circumstance.

Similarly, God is always at work within the hearts of those that believe (Philippians 1:6). Other people may judge that we're thriving or struggling based on what they see on the outside. But God cares about the inside, out of which everything else flows. Planted in His kingdom, our hearts are like a tree's center, growing inwardly so that all the goodness can flow outwardly to the tip of our tongue and to our hands and feet (Proverbs 4:23). It is our single-minded devotion to God that fuels a fruitful life in Him.

If you have a pet, odds are you have an excellent example of such loving devotion right in front of you. Every time the garage door opens, our mutt Millie leaps off the couch and sprints to the back entrance, tail wagging, hind body swaying, filled with expectant joy. She's fixated on one thought: "They're back!!" (as if we haven't reliably returned thousands of times in the same way before…). But her fierce loyalty is undeniably endearing, bidding us to stoop and rub her ears as we walk by or cup her face in our hands, stopping to say, "Hey Millie, how's my sweet girl!?"

Such a bond between dogs and their owners is not unusual. Famously, in Japan a professor used to take the train home every day. Stepping off onto the platform he was, like us, greeted by his dog Hachi bursting with joy at the sight of him. Like clockwork, they followed this routine, with Hachi arriving at Shibuya station at day's end in time

to make the walk home. With his thick peach-white fur, a full, curled tail and broad head, Hachi became a familiar sight at the station. But one day his owner did not return as usual. Not knowing the professor had passed away, Hachi nevertheless remained faithful. Every day for nine years, nine months and fifteen days (do the math, that's nearly 4,000 days!), Hachi returned to the station precisely at the time of the train's arrival in the hope of glimpsing his master again.

Another account (and by far a happier one) is the one of Bobbie the collie who got lost on vacation 2,500 miles from home. The amazing thing is that Bobbie then walked all the way back, from Indiana to Oregon, through snowstorms and wild terrain, across deserts, mountains and rivers.[25] It took 6 months (averaging 14 miles per day) but Bobbie made it back to his hometown – mangy, filthy and scrawny – where Nova, one of the two daughters, spotted him limping down the street: "Oh look! Isn't that Bobbie?!" Remarkably, the dog never gave up until he had found his way home.

The sixth Beatitude "Blessed are the pure in heart, for they will see God" asks us to have this same sort of singular devotion to God. It calls for us to have the type of love and zeal for the Lord that would compel us to meet Him every day, to wait for Him, to patiently endure silence or even trek through the wilderness (sometimes feeling totally lost) to get back to Him. Such a love is to drive our whole being, from our head to our tiniest toe, causing us to inwardly shake with excitement at the thought of being reunited with Him (Psalm 84:2). But unlike the Japanese professor, God will never not show up. And, unlike Nova, God will never be surprised we have returned. Instead, He will be waiting expectedly, with open arms, greeting us by name to lead us on the walk home.

To be "pure in heart" means to be "cleansed." But much more than that, it means to be undivided in our purpose to bring Him glory, and in our desire be a part of His kingdom (Psalm 86:11). When Jesus spoke of the "heart" it was much bigger than just gushy love stories or romantic, kissy-kissy feelings. It meant the *center* of the person. In the Bible, the heart is not just a stream of emotions but rather the fountain, the source, out of which the whole of YOU flows.

I try to tackle a sewing project occasionally. It's a dying art but I like to think I'm playing my minute role in keeping it alive, especially when I cajole my kids to join in. Though it may be a total grandma hobby, you can't argue it isn't useful: there are always hems to let down, shirts to mend and stuffed animals to repair. When I was young and thrifty, I even took on larger projects such as black-out lined drapes or fringed pillows. I learned through practice that square panels, perfect mitered corners and tight seams were born out of careful preparation.

"Inside out and right sides together is always how to start," my mom taught, for by sewing with the "pretty sides" touching, any seams would then be hidden and look nice from the outside when finished. "And remember, haste makes waste!" she'd always say, reminding me to take the time to flatten any folds or wrinkles before measuring, cutting or threading the fabric through the machine. Over and over, I'd run my palm to the edges so that the fabric was smooth and beautiful at the finish.

In our own hearts, the Lord is a master of handiwork, working to finish the good work He began in us. He is constantly preparing us, taking out any kinks and folds in our personality, any places where deception forms or hypocrisy

hides. He knows we struggle with double-mindedness, when we profess to live for Christ while still loving the world (e.g. "Can't we just have fun and save the church-stuff for later?"). He doesn't want us to show one side of ourselves to our family, then fold over a new side for our friends. In His hands, He makes our hearts straight and sincere, free from any idols or distractions that would ruin His design for a whole and beautiful, finished work. He's never hurried but orders every step, every stitch to perfection. And He always works from the inside out, knowing that true, lasting beauty is always fashioned in this way. We can come to Him like a heap of rags, and as long as we lay ourselves out before Him, He can use us for His glory.

Here again we see the clever parallels between the first four and last four Beatitudes (or specifically here between the second and sixth). Only by knowing how much I need Him to mend my messy, tangled heart (blessed are those who mourn), will I lay myself out before Him, asking Him to create in me an undivided, wholly devoted heart (Psalm 86:11). God knows change must start on the inside, for the heart is the center out of which all outward things flow (Matthew 15:19).

When asked by a Pharisee "What is the greatest commandment?" Jesus responded, "Love the Lord your God with all your heart and with all your soul and with all your mind" (Matthew 22:34-38 NIV). It doesn't work to be double-minded, serving the world and the Word. Just as the prophet Elijah challenged the people of Israel, "How long are you going to sit on the fence! If God is the real God, follow him!" (1 Kings 18:21), we must ask: "What am I holding back from God?"

Psalm 51:17 tells us that the Lord will never reject a pure and contrite heart. Such believers are eager for the Lord to work in them even though it can be difficult and painful at times. A contrite heart yearns to be truly mended, not just hastily pinned together by busyness, achievements, or good works, to look good from the outside. A heart that truly desires God isn't satisfied with eye-catching ribbons, decorations or easy iron-ons. Such things as good looks, big bank accounts or impressive résumés are things our world values. Though these outward things may look good for a time, they're not His design.

Case in point: compare the slightly built David who was God's choice of king with the tall and impressive Saul, the people's choice. No, there was nothing kingly about David from appearance. Quite the opposite: when the prophet

Samuel came to anoint a new king from among the sons of Jesse, they sent the youngest, David, to watch the sheep. "No chance *that* guy is the one!" they joked with a snicker. Everyone supposed it would be the stately, dignified brother, the one with the broad shoulders and handsome face, who would be chosen to lead.

But instead, after scanning and sorting through and finding no one suitable, Samuel called for the youngest to return from the pastures. The ruddy, small-framed David was far from ideal from the outside ("Wait, what, really … *this* guy?!) but the Lord knew David on the inside. "God judges persons differently than humans do. Men and women look at the face; God looks into the heart" (1 Samuel 16:7).

So exactly *how* are we to have a pure heart like David? Is it just a matter of working harder to be nicer, kinder, more polite, a tad bit friendlier and a smidge bit happier? Well, not quite … sheer effort won't get you there and will just leave you worn out (I know, I've tried it before). Remember, the Beatitudes aren't a list of to-dos or an instruction manual; they are a description of life in His perfect garden. God is the one doing the work of turning this wilderness into a new, restored creation, and we just have to be willing and responsive agents of His rule.

Understanding this, David fell before the Lord with this request: "Create in me a pure heart, O God, and renew

a steadfast spirit within me" (Psalm 51:10 NIV). After laying himself out before God, repenting for his sins (and yes, some things David did were downright dreadful), David pleaded for the Lord to continue His work within him. He asked Him to create a pure, unwavering heart, wholly devoted to God's ways. The "how" behind God's handiwork was to be plain and simple: "I keep my eyes always on the LORD," David said, "Day and night I'll stick with God" (Psalm 16:8).

But it takes effort to truly "see Him," to keep our eyes set on Him, as David did.[26] God, of course, is everywhere, always in front of us. He's in the sunset-streaked clouds, the flutter of birds' wings, or in the sound of river water lapping against the rocky shore. But to truly "see" God is on a different level.

Think of it this way. When we go to "see our grandparents," we don't just sit and stare at them across the dinner table. We chat, hug, remember, plan or simply enjoy being together. Likewise, "seeing God" requires engagement: talking with Him, interacting with Him, sitting with Him, and listening to Him. It can feel quite ordinary (don't look for Him to pop out of a burning bush or wave at you from the clouds), but no doubt He's working in extraordinary ways. Seeing God morning by morning, keeping Him right smack-dab in the center of our view, is the way we welcome God to give us a pure heart and work out His plan in us.

And "I will give you a new heart," God promises. "I'll remove the stone heart from your body and replace it with a heart that's God-willed, not self-willed" (Ezekiel 36:26). He'll iron out all the wrinkles, scrub out any stains and stitch it into an entirely new heart, from the inside out! And, most importantly, it's a NEW heart, not just a NICE heart. We ourselves can dial up niceness, crank up our efforts to be friendly, even-tempered and "a good guy" (we're quite good at making-do, pinning a seam, and even adding iron-ons, shiny rhinestones or fancy decals that pretty-up the outside). But it hardly lasts. Only God can create change that brings about a new heart – one that doesn't grow faint but grows in faith. In the words of C. S. Lewis, "God became man to turn creatures into sons: not simply to produce better men of the old kind but to produce a new kind of man."[27] Brand spanking new –not just twice as nice.

Even Christ, who we know was perfect, had to meet with God, listen to God and be taught by God. Incredible, right? Yes, it was His obedient attention and His prayers that *made* Him the perfect servant.[28] Morning by morning, the prophet Isaiah tells us, Christ was awakened to meet with God (Isaiah 50:4). And when God called, the Son cried out and kept His gaze on the Father. This is how Christ *learned* obedience and was *made* perfect (Hebrews 5:7-9). Does this mean that Christ was somehow disobedient before? No. It just means it didn't happen automatically, but He had to learn obedience through the things He suffered. This was real and authentic obedience. He prayed for strength and had to endure, just like we do, in order to whole-heartedly follow God.

This is how Christ ultimately became the second and true Adam – not like the first who hid when God called. No, the second Adam was one who listened and was willing to do anything to restore God's garden. This new Adam began the long-promised reversal to turn the wilderness of this broken world into a Garden-Paradise, renewing it person by person, tree by tree, until even the desert is a fruitful forest (Isaiah 32:15).

This brings me back to the rings of a tree's trunk. Peel away the bark of a tree and you will find a living document:

 a record of years of formation laid out in rings, each encircling the last. Every tree has its own unique design, like a fingerprint.[29] It's distinct and detailed, telling the tree's story. Wide rings indicate warmer, wet years and times of great growth; narrow rings tell of stressful conditions when the tree hardly grew at all.[30] But, no matter the circumstance, the progress is never half-way, notched or uneven, but always full circle to create a straight and strong supporting pillar. This innermost section of the trunk is – you guessed it – the *heartwood*.

We too sometimes experience years of great growth in our faith whereas other years feel spiritually dry. But as long as we stay centered, fixing our gaze on Him, He remains at work in the deep, private "insides" of our lives. He doesn't give up or skip over us or walk away. Despite our circumstances, He is always adding layers that run full circle, transforming our entire being. What we are at the invisible core (the heartwood) matters more to God than what we are at the visible branch.

And, like a tree's rings, God lays out His work in us in an entirely unique way. No two believers are exactly the same – we each have our own journey with Christ and we can't fully ever know anyone else's! C. S. Lewis' Christ-like figure Aslan explains it like this: "Child, I am telling you your story, not hers. No one is told any story but their own."[31] Because unseen by anyone else, the Father uniquely lays down every detail in our personal story. Like rings in a tree, they enable us to do the good work God set before us to do (Ephesians 2:10). And, amazingly, as part of God's kingdom, we can be used to play a part in the great rescue story that began with Christ.

We need just to look to Jesus for our example, whose life announced a new way of living in God's kingdom, as a tree of God's garden. In the Bible, Christ was often compared to a healthy tree – a green tree (Luke 23:31) and a growing vine (John 15:5). His heart was never divided, never wavering, but perfectly good. Unlike a dead, withering tree, He was a tree full of sap, fruitful in His preaching and teaching, rooted in God the Father. His heart was blameless, overflowing with grace and goodness.

But on the cross, this green tree, sturdy and strong, was nevertheless given over to be felled and cut off at the root. Remember Jesus' last words "My God, my God, why have you abandoned me?" (Mark 15:34). Christ, who could always see the Father morning by morning, day by day, took on our sin and, as a result, was split off from God. He was thrown out of the Father's garden so that that we may never be. Because of Jesus' sacrifice, we can now *always* see God and will one day fully see Him in all His glory. Christ paid the price for all our rottenness. And now in His garden, He gives the dead tree new life and makes the dry tree flourish (Ezekiel 17:24).

God's working hand never lets up but is always on our heart preparing us, making us new from the inside out as people of His eternal kingdom. So, we rejoice because we have been given a new heart. Once parched, dried-out and weary, we are now green and thriving, playing out our part of His plan to transform the whole earth from wilderness to garden, one tree at a time.

9

— THE WAY OF THE WOODS —

*Blessed are the peacemakers, for they will be
called children of God.*

Matthew 5:9 NIV

Only recently have we started to understand how trees in a forest behave and, quite remarkably, they are model peacemakers. Scientific discoveries have revealed that the way of the woods is not the cut-throat, "survival of the fittest" we were led to believe. Instead, it's like one big family, with each tree helping those around it to thrive. If a tree is sick, a neighboring, healthy tree can shuttle over water, carbon and nutrients like nitrogen through a vast system of fungi (mycelium) that connects them underground. By "sending signals" to their forest neighbors, one tree can feed, inform and support another.[32] And through these incredible below ground networks, mature trees can also help out the little guys, the nobodies on the forest floor, by sharing sugars produced in the leaves of their large canopies. They are willing to give, even when it's costly, to make peace with those around them.

So how does this vision of peacemaking translate into our own lives? World War I gives us a captivating example. Just imagine: it's five months into a grueling war and British and German soldiers have dug-in on opposite sides on the western front. They live for weeks in long, deep

earthen ditches, firing at each other night and day. Rats, lice, hunger and exhaustion are constant companions. Though it was Christmas Eve 1914, their spirits are at an all-time low, dampened by the realities of war and days of rain that soaked their bodies and the earth, creating a muddy, mucky mess.

But that very evening, the rain let up and a dazzling white crystal landscape formed across the entire battlefield. A hard freeze had turned the soggy grass into an icy frost that looked just like a sheet of diamonds all the way to the horizon. The men peered out from the trenches and leaned into the beauty and magic of the scene before them.

And then, something remarkable began to unfold...

Starting about 8:30 p.m., in an odd moment of joy, some soldiers broke out in song and lit lanterns, belting out at the top of their lungs entire stanzas of "Silent Night" and "The First Noel." The merriment grew as the night stretched on; for several hours the blast of enemy gunfire gave way to the sound of laughter. By dawn, men on both sides even began to climb out of the trenches. Literally hundreds from each side circled up in no man's land (the area between the two enemies) shaking hands, trading chocolates and cigarettes. A Scotsman appeared with a soccer ball and a game got underway, caps laid out as goals on the frozen ground.[33] Men, who only a day before were shooting at each other, were working together for a shot on goal.

That day, it could all have gone terribly wrong, but instead things went remarkably right – if only for a little while. No doubt each man took a risk, venturing out of their place of safety into plain sight, right in the path of an enemy bullet. It could have cost them their life. But that was the price of peace that halted a world war on Christmas Day and momentarily brought enemies together as friends.

In the seventh Beatitude, Christ is calling us into costly ventures to make peace among people. In His kingdom, peacemakers step out into no man's land, right into the place of hurt and hardship, to bring people together. Like the soldiers during the Christmas truce, peacemakers haul themselves out of hiding to stand on the frontline, looking for the middle ground. In Paul's words, God uses us as peacemakers to "persuade men and women to drop their differences and enter God's work of making things right between them" (2 Corinthians 5:19-20).

Instead of a battlefield, our no man's land is more likely to look like the hallway at school, the lunch table or the backseat of the car. And, instead of launching fire at another with a glance or smirky comment, we have the choice to lay down our defenses and climb out of our comfort zone to see things from the other person's point of view.

A peacemaker can do this — not because God made them nice or easy-going — but because God made them part of His family. The power is in being made new, as a son or daughter of Christ (hint: see earlier Beatitudes!). They have a pure heart, not cluttered by outside motives or hidden plans, and not at all distracted by thoughts such as: "When will I get my way?" "Is this good for me too?" They are dependent on God (poor in spirit) and can accept criticism (meekness) without getting bogged down in self-pity. They are okay with things not being okay because they know God will one day make all things good and right.

Quick note here: *peacemaking* is massively different from just *peacekeeping*. Peacemaking, which Christ calls us to, means doing the hard work of bringing people together. Peacekeeping, on the other hand, often just serves to keep people apart. Our worldly version of peace is sometimes just a feeble framework for *keeping* the peace that holds off conflict at arm's length with quick fixes. It applauds presidents, prime ministers and chancellors that pose together for TV, claiming "Peace for all!"

But Christ's version of peace is deeper and much more personal. It permeates every corner of His creation, playing out even in the fine texture of life, in our little day-to-day dealings with others. The peace Christ speaks of is the biblical concept of *shalom*, the Hebrew word for wholeness, harmony, and well-being. It means being right with God to therefore live right with others.

When Covid locked down our world in March 2020, everyone found themselves on strange little islands of isolation. Remember what it was like? No sports, no schools, no meals with friends or visits with grandparents. We grew distant from each other, like the unraveling of a long kite string in a gust of wind. And, suddenly, we were so far apart, there was no easy fix for reeling us back in. Many new issues kept us divided: masks, vaccines, quarantine. Attempts to get rid of the virus just seemed to make everyone even more upset.

Over months, the pandemic grew into a ruthless two-headed monster. It was like the Greek Hydra, that scary water serpent that re-grows two heads if you chop off the one. And so it went with Covid: we tried to kill the virus but instead it just grew a second head that spit anger into our communities.

We grew used to hiding and dodging the hard stuff, holing up at home, doing church online or logging on for virtual school. Like those WWI soldiers, it felt hard and risky to climb out of the trench. We were weary from a year of sickness, from uncertainty, from conflict and from constantly asking things like, "Can we go on that trip?" "Can I hug my grandparents?" "Can I blow out my birthday candles?" But, little by little, we went back to school, had people into our home and swapped Zoom meetings for real face-to-face conversation. By keeping in sight the end of the story – God's grand story – we were able to meet on middle ground and look back together, on the muck and messiness of our trenches.

Such peacemaking efforts always carry a cost. I'm not talking about dollars but sacrifices of the heart. It involves time and emotional energy listening to other points of view. When we ourselves are not getting along with someone, peacemaking might involve the pain of apologizing or confronting the person who's done the hurting. Other times, we find we must wait in nagging uncertainty, caught in a no man's land, until we can work out our differences and truly reconcile. In practical ways, we may have to risk some of our comforts to make time in an already packed schedule or be willing to host someone in our home (even when we'd rather have a laid-back movie night).

It would be a mistake to assume, however, that *costly* means *complicated*. Quite the opposite really – peacemaking efforts are usually quite simple. Maybe it means walking away from a conversation that is only stirring up drama. Maybe it's sending a text to ask, "Is everything okay?" Perhaps you bring someone a meal and make time to chat on their front porch. As we will see, Jesus, the model peacemaker, kept His efforts superbly simple, doing most of His peacemaking work around the table over an ordinary meal (like the Jesus-day equivalent of taco night or frozen lasagna). Even such a small

 gesture allows people to sit, talk, listen, build friendships and be at ease. Those very ordinary dinner parties, filled with the unlikeliest of guests, were exactly how Christ chose to show His people a little taste of the *shalom* of God.

We know Jesus could have worked miracles wherever and however He pleased. But we don't see Him negotiating a peace settlement between nations or shaking hands with officials. Instead, scripture tells us He chose to make peace in a much humbler setting usually gathered around a table. He was an exceptional host, gathering all types of folks to dine with Him (even though He likely never even owned a home!). This left many of His followers angry and confused. Because remember, his Jewish followers thought Christ came to re-arrange the table, to finally put them at the head (to be the big shots, the ones in-charge). But instead, Christ was busy *filling up* the table. He broke bread with Roman officials, the misfits and the marginalized, the riffraff and the rejected alike, to show they all had a part in His blessing (Matthew 11:19).

Today, you might hear adults smile and say, "Oh, isn't that nice!?" if their kid thinks to include that unpopular, sidelined classmate in their Friday night plans. But not so in Jesus' day – nothing cute about it. If you hung out with people outside of your religious circle, the Pharisees literally saw it as an act of defilement that made them unclean. In the first century, you never wanted to keep company with those "lower" than you. Meals continually reminded people "where they belonged," serving to bring people together or, more importantly, keep others out.

Knowing this, we can see Jesus' dinner parties were very risky affairs. It was a BIG deal that Jesus summoned Zacchaeus (the rich, crooked tax collector) to come down from the sycamore tree and have Him over for dinner (Luke 19). And it was a BIG deal that He welcomed a prostitute into Simon's home right in the middle of a dinner party with Pharisees (Luke 7)! Remember Levi, another crooked, despised tax collector? He certainly turned heads when he showed up for dinner at Christ's invitation (Mark 2:13-17), and later followed Jesus to become the disciple, Matthew! In every instance, Jesus didn't say "clean up your life and I'll accept you." Instead, He offered acceptance and made them feel they belonged. As a result, each unlikely guest felt cherished, not condemned, by their host and resultingly had a change of heart.

So, all happy endings, right? Not quite. Remember how the rest of the story went down? Did the *law keepers* and *law breakers* circle up and trade hugs and high fives? Did the Pharisees crawl out of their holy huddles, shake hands with the sinners, share their chocolates and join in the merriment? No! They sat in shock that Jesus was not the military leader they'd hoped for, but instead a warm, welcoming host to outsiders. They had hoped He'd unseat their enemies from places of power, but Jesus instead saved them a seat – at their table! The religious Pharisees retreated and muttered among themselves, "This man welcomes sinners and eats with them" (Luke 15:1-2). And they stayed in their trenches and plotted. Whenever they had the chance, they took shots at Jesus, falsely accused Him, and blamed Him.

Jesus knew He'd be killed for the company He kept, but His heart was for the "sin-sick, not the spiritually-fit" (Mark 2:17). He knew the cost. But He was acting out the BIG news of the gospel. Eating was a key way Jesus showed the love of God and announced the coming of His kingdom.[34] For Jesus, sharing a meal was never about filling bellies. It was a lavish act of peace that fed hearts and welcomed strangers, like us, to come, sit and be filled as part of God's family.

And Christ is still doing it – being the perfect host, reconciling people – all throughout the church. On Sundays, we go to a table during communion, remembering what Christ sacrificed to make us right with God and each other. We eat and drink with people, and all are "equal" before God. If Jesus' earlier meals with the marginalized and rejected were signs of the kingdom, how much more this one where people around the world come together!

This is what Jesus was hinting at all along: that one day all believers would be perfectly joined to God and each other.

And, again, as we have seen in previous chapters, the Bible is packed with garden and forest imagery to help us understand this truth of God's kingdom. Even those in Jesus' day would have taken note of scripture's use of tree imagery. For throughout the Old Testament, God's prophets (Amos, Jeremiah, Isaiah, Micah and Ezekiel) make abundant use of trees as a symbol of God's peace.

Now, thanks to the work of some curious scientists, we know trees are radically different than we supposed, adding fascinating depth to God's biblical imagery. We used to think that trees were utterly competitive, shading out their rivals, gobbling up sunshine and nutrients to cut out the little, young saplings scattered on the forest floor. But astoundingly, the forest is not a picture of competition but cooperation, with trees making peace with costly gestures.

It's as if they're seated at nature's table, feasting on CO_2, ample sunshine, and the things of the earth, and instead of throwing elbows and jockeying for position, the more mature trees are inviting the little guys in, sharing their portion and helping the least among them. And when things get hard maybe it's a storm, a fire, or a drought trees don't retreat, take cover or hole up (like we tend to do). Instead, they stand at-the-ready, firmly rooted right alongside their neighbor, connected through vast networks that keep them in-the-know about others' needs.

It's a fact: a seedling in the woods is four times (four times!) more likely to survive than a lone seedling planted off on its own.[35] The vast system of underground fungi which connects the trees to one another allows them to listen, respond and support each other, like one big family.

We too can stand together as a family, firmly rooted in Christ's love (Galatians 3:26; Colossians 1:20). Like the underground network of the forest, His love is far-reaching and works in unseen ways to bring us together. It's not anything of our own doing … it is the peace He gives to us as a gift of faith (Ephesians 2:11-22). That's why the risen Jesus greeted His disciples with the words "Peace be with you" (Luke 24:36; John 20:19). God is the one who opens our eyes and gives us the power to be a peacemaker so that grace and truth, like life-giving nutrients, spread where needed.

And in the end, ALL of creation will live in peace. Jesus, will finally host the feast He has been planning since the beginning of time: the grand wedding feast of the lamb, the awesome ending to His great rescue plan! Even the hard-to-see hurts among peoples will have been healed. Everyone who is in Christ will finally, perfectly be united at His table – the repentant tax collector and Pharisee, the lost and the weary, the humble and the pitied, laughing, singing, and delighting as guests of the Prince of Peace.

Would you be at all surprised if I told you this feast will take place at the foot of an enormous tree? This wondrous tree, we are told, bears a new kind of fruit each month and produces leaves that are used "for the healing of the nations." Scripture says the tree will grow on either side of the river of life for even the trees of the forest will be in perfect peace, acting as one (Revelation 22:1-2).

The whole scene is a beautiful reversal of sin's curse that separated us from God in the first place. For in the beginning, the eating of one tree broke our peace with God. We took its leaves to try to hide from God and from one another, no longer at peace with our Maker or His creation. But the eating of *this* tree will bring us life eternal, and its leaves promise to restore our peace with God and, in turn, with each other, forever. [36]

Blessed are those who are Persecuted because of Righteousness

10

— "REJOICE!" FOR — WINTER IS HERE

Blessed are those who are persecuted because of
righteousness, for theirs is the kingdom of heaven.

Matthew 5:10 NIV

Every year cool autumn breezes usher in lower temperatures and shorter days as the sun slips earlier and earlier below the horizon. All of nature can sense winter is drawing near. And like a warrior preparing for battle, trees make ready for the contest with their greatest enemy. They do not cower or shrink away from the punishing cold. Instead, they become *radiant*, bursting forth in brilliant displays of fiery reds, buttery yellows and blazing oranges. As if one big band of soldiers, the trees shout "Rejoice! Winter is upon us, but we are ready for battle!" And, likewise, by storing God's truth in our heart and being rooted in Him, we too can give a cheer when darkness is moving in. We can do this even when it means letting go of things that are precious to us.

For this reason, the Bible often portrays a believer in Christ as a warrior going into battle. We will, God warns, face losses and hard times simply for being a child of God. Of course, we are not *literally* going head-to-head in combat, but lots can be learned by leaning into this metaphor. In Jesus' day, Roman gladiators were the prime example of well-trained warriors. They were the portrait of purpose and  courage. They dressed in bronze armor with shiny silver helmets covering their heads, ears and jaws, and held sword and shield in hand. They fought for survival against other men, rhinos, lions and crocodiles in front of thousands, packed in arenas as large as college football stadiums![37]

When the gladiator strode out to meet his opponent, all eyes were on him. But you might be surprised that most of these "heroes" were the nobodies, with scarcely any rights or status in Roman society. [38] Their lives belonged to their masters. They fought, not because they wanted to, but because they had to. Their only chance at freedom was to persevere through many battles. So, after some big-time training, they stepped into the arena thinking about the life-after and the freedom and glory that could be theirs if they survived.

Likewise, Jesus wills us in this eighth and final Beatitude to step into the arena of faith. As believers, He warns: you WILL be thrown right in the middle of things. But train in the ways of His kingdom and look to the eternal reward promised! We are no longer slaves but sons and daughters armed with God-given tools: the belt of truth, the breastplate of righteousness, the shoes of the gospel of peace, the shield of faith, the helmet of salvation, and the sword of the Spirit (Ephesians 6:10-18). Take up your armor for the sake of God, our Father, who, unlike those Roman masters, never asks us to earn our freedom. Instead, He offers it as a free gift to all those that wrestle in this life for the glory to come.

But who and what exactly are we fighting against? Aren't God's people the kinds of people the world

wants? Who has any bone to pick with the pure, merciful peacemakers trying to make it right – aren't these the ones who will give up the front seat or share their last cinnamon roll? Doesn't the world want more of these "nice guys"?

But the Bible tells us a different story. The world is in rebellion against God. The darkness has always hated the light. Jesus Himself said that because He has chosen us out of this world, the world hates us (John 15:19). So, when someone comes along living out REAL loyalty to Christ, it rubs people the wrong way. It convicts them of their sin and makes them feel uncomfortable (John 16:8). Has that ever happened to you? For instance, if you are kind in a situation, someone who had been unkind will immediately feel guilty. If you act content, those that are grumbling and complaining will suddenly feel foolish. And, if you respond in humility, the prideful often feel deflated. In all these scenarios, others are left with an icky conscience – "Why is *that* guy not acting like everybody else?" The response: unbelievers often go on the offensive and try to knock us down, embarrass or defeat us (2 Timothy 3:12).

In this last and final Beatitude, unlike all the others, Jesus is not giving another description of His people but a dose of reality. He doesn't want us to feel surprised or discouraged when we encounter annoyance or even anger when we are living out the truths of His kingdom.

You remember how the Beatitudes can be divided into two sections, the first four and the last four? The first four describe a sort of emptiness (poor in spirit, mourning, meekness) that is then filled by a hunger for righteousness, that is, a desire to be Christ-like. The fullness that results is then described in the next three Beatitudes (the pure, the merciful, the peacemakers) whereby this Christ-likeness overflows for others. And what is the result? Surprisingly, it is persecution for this very righteousness. [39]

Now did you see it turning out this way? Love selflessly, serve others and you'll end up being put down and put out. Is that God's equation?! Doesn't sound like something we want to sign up for...

BUT Jesus bids us to not be so short-sighted. Look at the Beatitude as a whole: "Blessed are those who are persecuted because of righteousness, *for theirs is the kingdom of heaven*." It's like God's great drama is shown in two parts. In Part 1, the nice guy ends up losing, and you can't help but shake your fists at the TV saying, "That's not fair!" But then you watch the credits scroll and find there's a Part 2 – a brilliant Part 2 of the story to come! In this ending, all is made right, and you realize it's better than you could ever have imagined!

The same goes for those who are God's people fighting to be a light among the darkness. Whether they stumble or fall, make missteps or mistakes, Christ says "Rejoice!" for to them is given the *eternal* reward. It is the reward Christ promised with the very first Beatitude: "Blessed are the poor in spirit, *for theirs is the kingdom of heaven.*" For it all circles back to our primary and greatest reward to be with God just as He always intended it to be.

When I lived in Chicago in my early twenties, I was in a Bible study that met in one of the city's 180-some-odd Starbucks. This one was just north of downtown, tucked away in a strip mall. It had the usual green and white signage, display case with banana bread and cake balls and the sounds and smells of coffee, served hot, cold, whipped or frothed.

Five or six of us would gather there every Wednesday night to discuss a book of the Bible, huddled around a small table in the corner. Everything seemed pretty ho-hum and ordinary. So, it came at a surprise when my friend one night leaned over and in a soft voice asked "Are we allowed to do this? Talk about Jesus here?"

The question itself was telling. And it suddenly clued me into the unusual, unsettling vibe in the coffee shop. There were murmurs as people sipped and stared over the rim of their cups. The barista behind the counter looked like he wanted to ask us to leave. I felt exposed and embarrassed. I began to whisper the name "Jesus" lest someone might look our way again. But by now our faith was a scene and people couldn't help but judge. When we closed our eyes to pray, it felt like we were in one of those wax museums, frozen, on stage for others to point and stare at. They couldn't help but mutter to each other "Is that real or all just fake?"

We kept meeting there week to week, but the feeling we were in a fishbowl, being watched and critiqued, was changing us. Remaining steadfast even in the midst of small pressures (eye rolls, condescending looks) can strengthen your faith. We can feel very acutely we are His when we are suffering something big-scale (sickness, war, prison) but relying on Him when we feel irritated or annoyed matters as well. Sharing in Christ's sufferings means also holding up to frustrations on an average, windy, cold Wednesday night.

You see, when we talk about persecution, it tends to bring up images of being locked up in prison, thrown into the streets or beaten to a pulp. Extreme examples. But Jesus has a much broader definition. Look closely. He specifically includes verbal attacks, saying when "people put you down"

and later for emphasis in that same sentence "or speak lies about you to discredit me" (Matthew 5:11). So, persecution doesn't have be some bloody and gory scene. It includes those times when you feel left out, laughed at or judged on account of your faith – just like we felt in that coffee shop. In these moments, it will feel like you've been thrown in the arena and the large, watching crowd is your greatest opponent. All eyes will be on you, criticizing your every move, waiting for you to stumble.

When this happens what does Christ say? He says, "Rejoice! For you are being marked as My own." Just like valuable things are marked with a serial number (e.g. your phone, airpods, and Mac books marked by their creator "Apple"), we are marked as children of His kingdom.  The evidence is not inscribed on our arm or leg or ear but is a light within us. And you only know the light when it shines in the darkness. Try it: a flashlight shining on a sunny afternoon is hard to see but is nonetheless very impressive in a windowless closet. So, when you see your light against a dark backdrop, whether it be a nearly deserted coffee shop, the back of the bus or in the locker room, this is the moment for rejoicing, Christ says. Because that is the evidence that you belong to Him.

The eight Beatitudes Jesus spoke are some of the most well-known verses of the Bible. But they are also the most frequently misunderstood, and none more so than this last one! Here's why: people tend to like to leave out that all-so-important phrase "because of righteousness."

It's true we can go through a lot of rough times but it's not always "because of righteousness." Jesus is *not* promising we are always blessed when we are helpful or good or noble. He blesses those who suffer for *being righteous*, for acting like Him. So, for instance, this Beatitude does not apply those times we mutter to ourselves "Oh! I'm so glad I am so much better than everyone else, and that is why they don't like me." Don't laugh, you know you've done that before! We can be foolish and create a lot of difficulties for ourselves when we do things in a spirit of "Look how good I'm being!" We may choose a good cause like recycling or saving the pandas and preach it with such zeal that our friends grow annoyed and frustrated. This sort of persecution does not apply in this Beatitude. I'm not saying it's not good to stand for these things, but that is *not* what Jesus was talking about when he said "Blessed are those who are persecuted."[40]

Now knowing the difference – am I doing it for the sake of being good or for the sake of being like Jesus? – is not easy. It requires prayer and time in the scriptures. So let's take a look at some examples the Bible gives us.

Let's begin in the Old Testament. Do you remember the story of Daniel and his scary sleepover with the lions (Daniel 6)? Daniel quietly prayed to God three times a day behind closed doors and was thrown to the lions because there was a new law that forbade anyone from praying to God instead of the emperor (Daniel 6:7). By continuing to pray regardless, Daniel wasn't being difficult or showy or preachy. He was simply living out His love for God.

Moses also suffered much under Pharaoh's hand when he confronted him to lead God's people out of Egypt. And what did he find? More hardship! Forty years leading a bunch of hot, stinky and miserable folks to the Promised Land, a land that he himself would never see! But Moses, like Daniel, "had his eye on the One no eye can see, and kept right on going," looking ahead to his reward (Hebrews 11:26).

In the New Testament we see much persecution as well. Just look at God's warning to Paul when He chose him on the road to Damascus: "This man is my chosen instrument … I will show him how much he must suffer for my name" (Acts 9:15-16 NIV). And as Paul carried God's words to the

Gentiles, it happened just like that: multiple shipwrecks, arrests, imprisonment, beatings, and even a bite from a poisonous snake. But at the end of his life, Paul rejoiced, standing as a man in the arena who could confidently claim: "I have fought the good fight, I have finished the race, I have kept the faith. Now there is in store for me the crown of righteousness, which the Lord, the righteous Judge, will award to me on that day—and not only to me, but also to all who have longed for his appearing" (2 Timothy 4:7-8 NIV).

All of these characters in the Bible were persecuted, not because they were "good," but because they were *different*. Just looking at Jesus, wouldn't you say that is true of Him? He wasn't the most popular guy from Nazareth. The Pharisees hated Him because there was something about Him that made them cringe. His holiness convicted them. They felt unhappy because Jesus proclaimed that all their showy goings-on they worked so terribly hard at were for nothing. "Jesus has gone TOO far," they'd say, "to think, one only needs faith!" In essence, Jesus and His teachings were radically different from their laws and rituals. His very presence stirred the pot and made them angry.

Because of righteousness, Jesus was betrayed, beaten, bruised, battered and bound to the cross. Knowing all He'd face, in the Garden of Gethsemane He pleaded with

God to take away that suffering (Luke 22:39-46)! But rising out of this intense time of prayer, Jesus no longer showed any hesitation but perfect obedience. He could rejoice, for He knew there were better things waiting that would last forever (Hebrews 10:32-34). He never lost sight of where he was headed. For the joy set before Him, he endured the cross to end up *there*, in the place of honor, right alongside God (Hebrews 12:2 NIV/MSG paraphrased).

So when we're thrown in the arena, feeling beat down in front of a booing crowd, we can rejoice as Christ did! For it is "achieving for us an eternal glory" that far outweighs any of the troubles of this world (2 Corinthians 4:17-18).

Trees too face their own persecution: high winds, storms, pests, drought, and their greatest threat – winter. Sensing the dark, cold days approaching, they shed all their leaves and reduce themselves to their toughest parts: trunk, stems, branches and bark. But they don't just drop their leaves, feeling sad and sorrowful, shrinking and shriveling in the frigid air. No, quite the opposite! They rejoice.

They burst into a bold, radiant display, in all shades of crimson, amber, and gold. Entire mountainsides explode into color and even the solitary tree by the roadside becomes a thing to behold. They "give a cheer" the moment their strength is being tested (Matthew 5:11-12). Letting go and resting in God's plan set out before them, the trees are ready to take on winter's attacks. They endure, looking forward to the great bud burst of Spring, to a season of new life.

This is a clear picture of Jesus' words in the eighth Beatitude. Persecution and hardship are as unavoidable as the coming of winter every year, but we can rejoice even in those darker days knowing that a season of abundant light and life has been promised to us.

As a boy, and then a young man, Jesus too knew a dark season was ahead. For roughly three years, He would be in the arena, doing God's work. He would preach and teach the ways of God's kingdom, absorbing the insults of a riotous crowd until, ultimately, they crucified Him. But Scripture tells us that at Christ's baptism, right before His ministry would begin (*right* before He would encounter Satan himself in the wilderness), the Father and Son remarkably rejoiced together!

After Jesus waded in the Jordan River to be baptized, we are told the heavens opened and the Spirit of God shone down on Him. This was the moment Jesus stepped center-stage to do the Father's work. And as a result, we are told He was radiant, bathed in a brilliant light. "Beads of water glittered and sparkled like tiny diamonds in His hair."[41] Christ was about to face THE enemy but it was as if God said, "Wait! This is a time to rejoice!" God literally spoke from the heavens, "This is my Son, whom I love; with him I am well pleased" (Matthew 3:17).

When we suffer for His name, whether in small or mighty ways, God proclaims the same words of approval over us. He does so clearly and loudly, delighting in the work we are doing in His name. For we are a light, shining like a multitude of golden autumn leaves flickering in the sunshine, rejoicing in the promised glory that is to come.

11

— CONCLUSION: —
LIVING AS OAKS OF RIGHTEOUSNESS

id you know there are more trees on earth than there are stars in the galaxy?[42] It is as if at every turn God has placed a reminder, a guidepost for how we are to live in His kingdom. As we ride to school or work, we see hundreds of trees firmly rooted by the roadside, in our neighborhood and in the green spaces beyond.

Each is slightly different from the other, of different ages and stages, sizes, circumstances, and strengths. They, like us, are varied but, in every case, their beginning was humble and small, as they burst through the hard shell of a tiny seed. Over time, the trees grow inwardly and then flourish outwardly, helping

those around them and enduring - even rejoicing in the midst of - bitter storms and harsh seasons for the promise of new life and renewal.

We too as God's people are scattered all over the earth. Whether we put down our root in cities, suburbs or little-known places, we are signs and symbols for what life looks like planted in God's kingdom. God is using *us* one by one to transform the wilderness back into His garden. We are God's agents doing His work in His kingdom.

As we conclude, it is worth re-emphasizing that the Beatitudes are not a list of to-dos but rather a picture of a life in Christ. In each of the eight Beatitudes "Christ is not telling us what we should be. Rather He is describing what the power of God's kingdom makes us."[43] And this power works in direct conflict with the values of the world. Even the way we grow is counter-cultural - it's not by trying harder but by submitting to His will for our lives. By following Him, we find life is not about striving for status but striding with the Spirit.

Realizing that moment is a lot like learning to ride a bike. At first, it seems as if a force like gravity is always  pulling you in the opposite direction. Just staying upright is the challenge – any little obstacle makes your fingers curl over the brakes, feet slide on the pavement. You feel uncertain and unsteady. The result: skinned knees, nicked handlebars and banged up pedals. It feels foreign and hard to "go all in." But you keep being drawn back to keep on trying, perhaps as others cheer you on. Then, one glorious day (legs pumping, the wind in your face), it finally clicks. The way forward is obvious and there's no going back. It suddenly seems effortless as the wrestle with gravity has been won. It happens in just a moment, but everything is different. And though you'll still run into some tricky spots, staying upright is no longer the challenge.

This moment is akin to the moment we give our life to Christ. We take root in His garden kingdom. And by trusting in Him, we discover we have the hand of God steadying us, the wind at our backs, pushing us ahead with purpose. We follow a path cut just for us, leading to where God would have us. As one famous Christian writer put it: "The easiest thing in the world is to be a Christian …The Christian life is in balance with all of creation." [44] Of course, there will always be that other force tugging at us, trying to pull us down; but with God we have triumphed over it.

We can be sure of this because of what Christ has done. He is both the garden gate and the Gardener, welcoming us back into His presence where death, sickness and all evil have been defeated. Born out of a stump, the humblest of all servants, He surrendered to the Father's plan for Him (Isaiah 11:1). He was mocked, ostracized and criticized for loving the poor, the meek, and the undeserving. Then, He died on a tree, feet and hands nailed to the wood. Christ was totally uprooted and thrown out of God's kingdom so that we could be firmly replanted in God's garden. In His resurrected body, He now sits at the right hand of the Father, tending to and interceding for His followers.

One day, scripture promises, we will live in this garden for eternity where we will be saturated in His love, fixed forever by a stream of life-giving water. For now, we live as "oaks of righteousness, a planting of the Lord for the display of his splendor," in the new-Eden God is building *right now* for eternity (Isaiah 61:3). "My kingdom is Here!" He has declared. And by working in the hearts of you, me, and all believers, He is slowly but graciously turning the wilderness of this broken world into a Garden-Paradise for eternity.

So, take root in Him and grow, for your life is unfolding His Grand Story to restore everything just as He created it to be.

— WHY WRITE? —
(FOR ADULTS AND CURIOUS KIDS)

I think of my own children growing up in this fast-paced culture of instant gratification, novelty, catchy hashtags … and it's easy to see how the long-viewed calling of the Christian life is tossed aside like last year's Legos. Once neatly packaged, glossy and new, it's riveting. But, after completing the checklist in the instruction manual, the set loses its luster and sits like a relic in the corner of the bedroom. Likewise, we tour through the Bible with our young ones as if flipping through a guidebook, taking in the high points. And then it's set aside.

They grow up, go to school, and get busy, and the call to the road of faith becomes something they must respond to on their own. We pray they understand being a Christian is not just a declaration of faith, but a lifelong process of following the example of Christ.

And so as parents we find, as Eugene Peterson observed, it's not difficult to get a person interested in the gospel, but

it is "terrifically difficult to sustain the interest."[45] Every child is ultimately the work of God; but what is our role in propping up, watering and fertilizing these saplings of the Spirit?

As a mother of three, the answer to the above could begin to feel like another "to-do." But the power of the Scripture is that it is promises life-giving change through the work of the Spirit. So my role seems to be to just make the words of Christ more accessible and relevant for each of my children.

Three things happened, all about the same time and all involving books, that brought about the idea for *this* book. First, we were in the middle of a global pandemic and the volume on our world had been dialed down. Schools closed, sports leagues cancelled, church services went virtual. I searched for books to give my older children, then ten and eight, that shared biblical truths. Books, after all, are an introvert's best friend and my two were definitely on the quieter side. Suggestions ran the spectrum from Sally Lloyd-Jones' *Storybook Bible* and Tim Keller's short read *The Freedom of Self-Forgetfulness.* Both are phenomenal takes on the gospel and Christian-living but one came off too "childish" for their liking and the other was decisively too "grown up." What we were lacking was something in the middle, a book that had a mature tone and yet used illustrations that spoke to their life (scenes of school, sports, sweets!).

Second, I was reading John Mark Comer's *The Ruthless Elimination of Hurry*, and the following quote was stirring in my mind:

> "At the end of the day, what a post-Christian world is making us do is get back to the basics—apprenticeship to Jesus. The basic, countercultural, revolutionary lifestyle of Jesus."[46]

I was reflecting on this as I tidied up my son's room, squaring off a stack of *Who Was* books on his nightstand:

Who Was Theodore Roosevelt, Who Was Steve Jobs, Who Was Dr. Seuss. The tower was a monument to mankind, recounting our own history of accomplishments and achievements written from a secular perspective. These books offered a sharp contrast to Comer's challenge to live a life in apprenticeship to Jesus. Though good and heroic, these

stories mirrored our culture's fixation on *success* versus *fruitfulness*. I wanted my children to absorb the means and ends of the latter, a life lived to the fullest in the kingdom of God. I wanted them to understand it is not about what you do, but what God has done.

That was the third and final moment, when the idea for this book broke through. As adults, we have libraries of theological books to help interpret the Word. We are aided in our decision to walk in His ways. But what's out there for a tween/teenager to learn more about how Christ wants us to live?

It seemed a gap was being uncovered. Sunday school and large group ministries do an amazing job freshly packaging the gospel, making it feel alive, new, and life-giving once again to tweens/teens. But it can also be exhausting, hard and draining for 30-50% of those kids that identify as introverts. Susan Cain's 2012 work on introversion is now helping to address how our schools and places of work limit introverts' engagement, but what are we doing as a church? Not just on Sundays but as the larger, universal Church to reach these quieter children "who are most alive when things are a little bit quieter and more mellow."[47] One might conclude there's not a market for religiously themed books among tweens, but I'd argue from Cain's research that the assumption is illogical because it stems from a broad culture (including the church) that prefers extroverts. I believe those quieter-minded kids are out there.

So, this is written for the "saplings" among us – the tween/teenagers in the church. By reading this book, kids will get a better understanding of what it means to live like Christ and grow rooted in His kingdom, here in the now. After all, equipping ourselves with such a mind like Christ is a life-long endeavor that can be begun at any age. Christ's example and the truths in the Beatitudes are a counter-cultural presentation to notions of ambition, power and comfort that prevail today just as they did in the first century.

Sheer grit or stick-to-itiveness did not drive this project, but rather a sort of relenting and slowing down. I read, observed and listened more. I prayed. I wrote hemmed in by the ordinary: between laundry, meal prep, school drop-offs, church meetings, walks with the dog and talks with my kids. And it was on these ordinary walks and drives that He kept showing me little windows into His kingdom through the beauty and life of trees. It kept me writing even when I felt discouraged. And so, I gingerly lay out this book, praying God will use it to stir truth in the hearts of readers, as it did in mine.

As Paul noted in Philemon verse 6, sharing our faith has a way of deepening our own understanding "of every good thing we have in Christ." The Lord has graciously shown me things each time I put my fingers to the keyboard. And for that I will be eternally grateful, no matter if these pages are read by 10, 110 or 10,010 people. Because whether this book serves to tend a few trees, or many, it will be just as the Great Gardener would have it.

— END NOTES —

Chapter 2: Seeds of Faith

1   Lewis, C.S. letter to Mary Willis Shelburne, June 28, 1963, in the collected
     letters of C.S. Lewis, vol 3: Narnia, Cambridge and Joy, 1950-1963, ed.
     Walter Hooper, San Francisco: Harper San Francisco, 2007.

2   Lewis, C. S. *The Great Divorce.* New York: Collier Books, 1984.

3   Carey, Jim. Speech at 2016 Golden Globes.

4   Heimel, Cynthia. *If you Can't Live Without Me, Why Aren't You Dead Yet"* New
     York: Grove, 1991, p. 13-14.

5   Lewis, C.S. *Surprised by Joy.* New York, Harper Collins: 1998.

6   Spurgeon, Charles. "Supposing Him to the Be Gardener," sermon. Dec.
     31, 1882.

Chapter 3: Life from Barren Branches

7   Spurgeon, Charles. "The Beatitudes," The Charles Spurgeon Sermon
     Collection:
     https://www.thekingdomcollective.com/spurgeon/sermon/3155

8   Zetlin, Minda. "11 Ways to Make Yourself Happy Everyday," Inc.com:
     https://www.inc.com/minda-zetlin/11-simple-ways-to-make-yourself-
     happy-every-day.html

9   Peterson, Eugene. *Run with the Horses.* Illinois: InterVarsity Press, 2019.

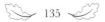

Chapter 4: Bending, not Breaking

10   Kemp, Anna. *Rhinos Don't Eat Pancakes*. New York: Simon and Schuster, 2011.

11   Buzzeo, Tony. *One Cool Friend*. New York: Dial Books, 2012.

12   Lloyd-Jones, D. Martyn. *Studies in the Sermon on the Mount*. Grand Rapids, MI: Wm. B. Eerdman's Publishing Company, 1976.

13   Lewis, C.S. *Mere Christianity*. New York: Harper One, 2001.

Chapter 5: Expansive Roots

14   Lewis, C.S. *Mere Christianity*. New York: Harper One, 2001.

15   Keller, Timothy. "Meditation: Psalm 1" podcast. *Gospel in Life*. Nov. 3, 2020.

Chapter 6: Intermission

16   Lloyd-Jones, Martyn. *Studies in the Sermon on the Mount*. Grand Rapids, MI: Wm. B. Eerdmans Publishing Company, 1976.

Chapter 7: The Giving Tree

17   Ten Boom, Corrie. *The Hiding Place*. Grand Rapids, MI: Chosen, 2006.

18   Ibid

19   Lewis, C.S. *Essay on Forgiveness*. New York: MacMillan Publishing Company Inc., 1960.

20   MacArthur, John. *The Only Way to Happiness: The Beatitudes*. Chicago: Moody Press, 1998.

21   Keller, Tim. "The Grace of the Law," sermon. Jan. 1, 2009.

22   Keller, Tim. "Mercy Not Sacrifice," sermon. Sept 17, 1995.

23   "How Trees Work for Us – Take a Look!" Borelforest.org

24   Sleeth, Matthew. *Reforesting Faith.* New York: Waterbrook, 2019.

Chapter 8: Tree Ring Patterns

25   "Grave of Bobbie the Wonder Dog," Roadside America.

26   Keller, Tim. "Integrity." Sermon. Gospelinlife.org (accessed March 18, 2021).

27   Lewis, C.S. *Mere Christianity.* New York: Harper One, 2001.

28   Motyer, K. Alec. *The Prophecy of Isaiah: An Introduction and Commentary.* Illinois: InterVarsity Press, 1993.

29   Gramlin, Carolyn. "Tree Story Explores What Tree Rings Can Tell Us About the Past," *Science News*, June 1, 2020.

30   "What Can Trees Tell Us About Climate Change?"NASA *Climate Kids*, https://climatekids.nasa.gov/tree-rings/. (accessed Dec. 23, 2021).

31   Lewis, C.S. *The Horse and His Boy.* New York: Harper Trophy, 1982.

Chapter 9: The Way of the Woods

32   Simard, Suzanne. TED Talk. "How Trees Talk to Each Other." June 2016.

33   Dash, Mike. "The Story of the WWI Christmas Truce." *Smithsonian Magazine*. www.smithsonianmag.com (accessed July 18, 2021).

34   Smith, Gordon. *A Holy Meal: The Lord's Supper and the Life of the Church.* Michigan: Baker Academic, 2005.

35   Simard, Suzanne. TED talk. "How Trees Talk to Each Other." June 2016.

36   Mounce, Robert H. *The Book of Revelation, The New International Commentary on the New Testament.* Grand Rapids, MI: Wm. B. Eerdmans Publishing Co., 1997.

Chapter 10: "Rejoice!" for Winter is Here

37   www.thecolesseum.org

38   Ibid

39   Piper, John. "Blessed are the Persecuted." sermon: March 16, 1986.

40   Lloyd-Jones, Martyn. *Studies in the Sermon on the Mount.* Grand Rapids, MI: Wm. B. Eerdman's Publishing Company, 1976.

41   Lloyd-Jones, Sally. *The Jesus Storybook Bible.* Grand Rapids, MI: Zonderkidz, 2007.

Chapter 11: Living as Oaks of Righteousness

42   "My Passion for Trees," BBC One, 2017.

43   Ferguson, Sinclair. *The Sermon on the Mount: Kingdom Life in a Fallen World.* The Banner of Truth Trust, 1987.

44   Peterson, Eugene. *A Long Obedience in the Same Direction: Discipleship in an Instant Society.* Downers Grove, Illinois: IVP Books, 2019.

Notes: Why Write?

45   Ibid, p. 10.

46   Pastor, John J. Interview with John Mark Comer, "Pastoring Portlandia," Oct. 25, 2016.

47   Cain, Susan. *The Power of Introverts in a World that Can't Stop Talking.* New York: Crown Publishers, 2012.